JOSEPHINE BAKER

Biography

Banana Dance and the Theatre Revolution

TABLE OF CONTENTS

Introduction

1 - FROM THE BANKS OF THE MISSISSIPPI TO THE BANKS OF THE SEINE

Childhood and Beginnings

2 - PARIS NEWS AND VIEWS

3 - FIRST TOUR OF THE OLD AND NEW WORLDS

4 - A CINEMATIC TURN

5 - AN ENORMOUS APPETITE AND SOFT SKIN

An Offering of Recipes

6 - HOW I BECAME A SINGER

From Rue Pigalle to the Club des Champs-Élysées, and Cabarets

7 - FROM THE STAGE TO THE GRAMOPHONE

From Negro Songs to "Ave Maria"

8 - FOUR YEARS OF ADVENTURE

In the Service of France on the Sidelines of the Second World War

9 - SECRETS FROM THE BOUDOIR

Jo and Jo

10 - A FINAL WORD ON THE CELEBRITIES OF THE TIME

Introduction

Meeting Josephine Baker

Josephine Baker erupts in hilarity when I initially proposed that she compose her memoirs in late 1926. A tranquil guesthouse near Parc Monceau in Paris was where she resided, having recently turned twenty. Josephine was still unconscious, despite the fact that it was midday.

"Oh, there is no need for concern; you were correct to awaken me!" She exclaimed, bounding over a small bench and extending an invitation for me to sit.

We conversed in English, as she was only familiar with a few French terms, including "bonjour," "bonbon," and "Champs-Élysées." She was tall, slender, full of energy, and prone to mirth, dressed in a pink dressing gown and matching babouche slippers. Her magnetic presence was further enhanced by her slicked-back hair, silver nails, and dazzling eyes.

"Memoirs?" However, I have yet to recall my own recollections. She chuckled.

While I awaited the interpreter who arrived late, I observed the room: a birdcage situated adjacent to a bust of Louis XIV, a rag doll perched on an Empire-style cabinet, a gramophone that was prepared to be played, and a mound of one-hundred-franc notes in the vicinity.

She stated, "Paul Colin requested that I compose a preface for Le

Tumulte Noir." "Consequently, I selected a pen and, in an instant, composed a narrative on two blank sheets." It was enjoyable! However, I would not undertake the same course of action in the future.

The question is, "Why not?"

"You are incomprehensible!" Writing by me? I am a performer. I am passionate about dancing; it is the sole activity that I aspire to pursue, and I will continue to dance until my death.

She sank into a leather armchair, her head resting on her shoulders and her eyes closed. Suddenly, she launched a slipper into the air with a laugh.

"Indeed, it is impossible." However, if you wish, I could recount my anecdotes, and you could compose my memoirs. What about that?

"We could accomplish that."

"Excellent!" I was conceived on the Mississippi River's banks... Oh, my animals are in such a state!

A pounding on the door. The telephone sounded. Seeds were inserted into Louis XIV's nostrils by the budgies.

A Phenomenon: Josephine Baker

Josephine Baker's dance, voice, and sheer presence mesmerized audiences on European stages and in music venues. Our encounters spanned decades, from the sensational La Revue Nègre in 1925, during which she danced in a mere banana belt, to her metamorphosis into an international French icon.

It was on a Tripcovich cargo ship in late 1925 that I first learned of her, as a radio officer extolled the virtues of "Josephine Baker—the revelation of Paris." I subsequently read a Candide review by Pierre de Régnier, in which he described her explosive performance at the Champs-Élysées as a whirlwind of energy, a body that moved like a live saxophone, and a dancer who defied definition.

La Revue Nègre, similar to the Ballets Russes, elicited both admiration and outrage; however, it also introduced a novel artistic form. Josephine Baker was a living poetry.

Although I was unable to attend the original revue, I still have vivid memories of the resounding ovation that greeted her upon her return to Folies Bergère.

Beyond the Stage—A Call to Action

Josephine Baker was not merely an entertainer. She was a lieutenant in the French military during World combat II, where she served in intelligence and provided care for thousands of combat orphans.

She declined publicity for her charitable endeavors. Each evening, she hurried to Gare du Nord after her performance to provide assistance to refugees. She fed children, provided solace, and organized aid parcels for soldiers.

She was gravely ill in Casablanca by 1942, but she remained resolute: "Keep your spirits up!" she wrote to me in a dispatch. She resumed her duties after months of recuperation, entertaining French troops in Sicily, Egypt, and throughout North Africa.

General de Gaulle personally recognized her devotion by composing a handwritten letter of admiration.

Multiple Lives of Josephine Baker

Every few years, Josephine Baker's existence underwent a transformation, revealing new facets of her talent:

In 1925, the Black Venus was at the pinnacle of jazz, captivating and shocking audiences.

She transforms into a European superstar at Casino de Paris in 1930, no longer a passing phenomenon.

1935 – She develops into a complete artist, transitioning from dancing to singing, and then from vocals to film and theater.

1940 – She commits herself to the French Resistance, viewing the conflict as a crusade against racism.

In 1945, her performances were transformed into tragediennes of the music hall, as a result of the refinement she underwent as a result of her wartime experiences.

However, she would continue to assert that her internal conflicts would never cease, even after she had conquered the globe. A coquette with a heart of gold, Josephine Baker remained a straightforward, free-spirited, and enigmatic woman beneath all the fame.

Josephine Baker: A Life of Contrasts

Madame Jean Lion was the name that Josephine Baker assumed in 1937. She married Jo Bouillon a decade later. She returned to the United States after a twelve-year absence, only to encounter the prejudice she had previously managed to avoid. Despite her status as a decorated French lieutenant and international celebrity, she was compelled to travel in segregated train carriages. She was denied a room at the Waldorf Astoria in New York, as there were no accommodations available for colored citizens.

As one chooses freedom, Josephine had selected France, and she harbored no resentment in spite of the injustices. She desired to abandon prejudice and embrace only music, dance, and pleasure.

"Do you recall the content I composed for Paul Colin's portfolio, Le Tumulte Noir?" Let us return to that.

She recalled the era in Paris when Black culture was a source of fascination, similar to the Charleston craze. She recounted a whimsical narrative about a visit to a friend's residence, where disorder prevailed—a cat suspended from the chandelier, overturned cages, and broken dinnerware. In the midst of a playful argument, the couple requested her assistance in resolving a disagreement: "Josephine, which is correct?" She merely advised them to remain composed, unaware of their argument. In the end, they admitted that they had been dancing the Charleston. In order to maintain harmony, she declared them both to be correct.

Queen of the Spectacle

It was now March 1949. Josephine was in her dressing room, preparing for Féeries et Folies at the Folies Bergère, where she portrayed both Joséphine de Beauharnais and Mary, Queen of Scots.

Jean Barreyre, a theater critic, described her as "a princess of the pose, an empress, with the grace of a hummingbird and a voice that sings to the heart." She is not only dominant on stage due to her height, but also because of her talent, which emanates compassion. She is an unparalleled celebrity, her silver-lined eyes brimming with emotion as she expresses her gratitude to the audience.

"What do you say to continuing these memoirs, José?" I inquired.

"All right, but let us concentrate on the enjoyable aspects, including those that stem from the war." Even in the horror, there were numerous humorous instances. Ah! Is that acceptable?

Josephine was a kind and generous individual who was cherished by both her younger and older counterparts. She provided assistance to numerous individuals in need; however, she declined to engage in conversations regarding her charitable organization. She had accumulated millions of dollars in debt after the conflict, and she had to pawn her jewelry to support her causes. "That is my responsibility," she declared. "I was obligated to do so."

She altered the topic with a mischievous smile. "Are you composing today?" Alright. Find a position. Certainly! To begin with, that day, I plunged into the sea...

A Life Narrated in Moments

These memoirs are not a linear narrative; rather, they are a compilation of defining moments that span more than two decades. They constitute a portrait of a woman that Paris had immortalized—once frenetic, now almost regal, but always profoundly affecting.

1

FROM THE BANKS OF THE MISSISSIPPI TO THE BANKS OF THE SEINE

Childhood and Beginnings

St. Louis and My Origins

St. Louis is a vast, frigid city that is home to 800,000 individuals, 100,000 of whom are Black. The Mississippi, which is laden with yellow muck, flows through its center, concealed by the thick black smoke of cotton-laden flatboats and paddleboats en route to the ocean. The Seine is essentially a stream in comparison to it. The city is crisscrossed with railways and factories, their chimneys staining the sky, and a towering bridge rises above the river.

Wood, grain, flour, engines, cotton, and maize are all sold in St. Louis. In the past, they even traded furs. The city was established by the French; detailed information is available. I was born on Bernard Street on

June 3, 1906—a beautiful and very amusing place.

My family was composed of my mother, grandmother, great-grandmother, sibling, and two sisters. My father was employed at a remote location. My mother and he had met at school, married against the desires of their families, and were subsequently left without support. In order to survive, they dispersed, with each individual attempting to support themselves. I recall that my mother resided with my grandmother, who was extremely impoverished. We encountered significant difficulties during our childhood.

My father and sisters were employed when my great-grandmother and grandmother died away. And I? Furthermore, I increased my workload. I was the "big man" of the household.

School and the Passion for Learning

Starting school at the age of five, I was never able to maintain my attendance. I engaged in arguments with both students and instructors, as I loathed being directed. Furthermore, they prohibited me from exhibiting amusing facial expressions; however, why should they remain static? Facial expressions are a sport that is equally significant as any other.

I developed into an excellent student in spite of the physical altercations and penalties. I particularly enjoyed studying history. It continues to captivate me. I am interested in learning about the actions of individuals of all races throughout history. I admired the manner in which history texts illustrated the evolution of clothing from one page to the next.

I was preoccupied with the subject of monarchs and queens at that time. Every night, I dreamed of them, imagining their golden robes trailing behind them like roads. However, in my visions, their staircases were infinite, and they never reached me. Later, I discovered that certain monarchs were cruel. That astounded me. A king? What is the average? That is not acceptable! I desired to combat all individuals who cause harm to the impoverished, regardless of their status as a monarch.

The Reason for My Career as a Dancer

I became a dancer due to my birthplace in a cold city, my infancy spent in shivering, and my unwavering desire to perform on stage.

Before I reached the age of ten, I constructed a small theater in the cellar of my mother's residence in St. Louis. Candles were positioned on empty New Zealand peach cans to illuminate the pathway, while the curtain was constructed from stitched-together remnants. The children from the community, who comprised the audience, were seated on an old bench and crates.

I was the focal point. I was enveloped in the fabric of my mother's oversized dress, as if I were a prisoner in a pillowcase, and I wobbled in her high heels. One pin was required to be paid in order to enter my theater.

A performance was held each evening.

Until one evening, the candles ignited my dress. The audience dispersed. I was alone with the flames. I scarcely succeeded in removing the dress in time. Just in time.

A Passion for Animals

I have always harbored an affection for creatures, including monkeys, parrots, dogs, cats, and snakes. Every creature that I discovered that was abandoned I carried home. My mother also enjoyed them; however, she disposed of them when they became excessively numerous. I subsequently followed suit. She would not permit them to enter the bedroom, so I frequently slept in the cellar with my canines and cats, hosting informal tea parties for them.

However, rodents have never been my favorite animal. Born with raw, tailless epidermis, hypocrites. I observed as they crept, halted, listened, and then vanished, only to reappear.

Leaving School at the Age of Eight

When I was eight years old, I opted to leave education in order to pursue employment. Mama was the sole individual earning a meager income, and we were both famished and cold. My relative, who was more affluent than Mama, secured employment for me, primarily in the care of white children in affluent households. They were fragrant, delicate, and warm. Additionally, I assisted in the kitchen, conducted errands, and cared for dogs. I cherished every aspect of it.

Subsequently, tragedy struck.

They carried home a small, white chicken named Jacki from one residence. We developed a friendship. I was aware that he loved me, despite the fact that his golden eye appeared to taunt me. I tended to him until he developed a robust physique, his pink headpiece shining with pride.

Then, one morning, the woman of the house weighed him, turned to me, and said, "Kill him."

I pleaded and cried, but she threatened to terminate my employment without compensation. Mama, my siblings, and my severe aunt were all in my thoughts.

Consequently, I executed the task.

I held Jacki upside down, turned away, and—bam—I severed his trachea. He let out a shriek. Blood spurted forth. His life was sliding through my fingers as his body thrashed.

I fled home without any money, anticipating that I would be subjected to a thrashing for failing to return with it. However, I never returned to that residence. I never mentioned it again.

Dolls, animals, and colors

Currently, I possess seven dogs, three cats, a monkey, a parrot, two budgies, three white mice, a goldfish, and a serpent that coils on the floor in a manner reminiscent of a signature. The reason I am fond of animals is that they are both straightforward and complex, much like children.

I once owned a pig named Albert, who wiggled his buttocks like a ribbon and waddled sideways. On the other hand, cats are fond of human sweat; they consume old garments by shredding them.

Additionally, I possess an affection for figurines. They are devoid of bones and resistance. I depict them in every conceivable manner, from drenched in color to draped in tatters. I am particularly fond of the company that produces dolls and creatures.

A Child Without Stockings

I attended dance performances at the Booker T. Washington Theatre on Sundays for a mere fifteen cents. Despite my aversion to ballet, I meticulously examined each and every movement. The dancers on pointe appeared ridiculous—pip, pip, pip—like small birds in wispy dresses. Insanity.

I was perpetually chilled. In order to maintain my body temperature, I engaged in dancing.

I also had a fondness for disguises. I dressed up as various individuals in order to observe the outcome, ringing doorbells and scurrying away when someone grinned at me.

1st Trip—Philadelphia

I accompanied my grandmother, a proud woman in grand dresses, large hats, and gigot sleeves, on a trip to Philadelphia when I was ten years old. She donned a hat with a central hole, but her bun was never able to fit through it. People turned and laughed as she walked.

We distributed a single embroidered petticoat among our three daughters on Sundays. I primarily walked barefoot. I once trod on a rusty nail, which caused my heel to swell. The physician contemplated amputating my foot.

Subsequently, they redirected me to school in order to prevent me from roaming the streets. However, I continued to engage in dress-up activities on Thursdays and Sundays.

One day, I donned my grandmother's dress, which featured a train and synthetic red hair. The hat—oh, the headgear! I require a moment of mirth.

The Initial Steps on Stage

I was under the supervision of my aunt when I performed in a theater on Mondays and Fridays at school. I did not participate in any rehearsals. I simply allowed the music to guide me.

I consistently asserted that I was elder than I actually was. This was the method by which I earned nine dollars per week when the revue was not in a state of decline.

I was nearly as tall and robust as I am now at the age of sixteen.

My hair was subsequently trimmed.

I also departed from my family.

"You can't do anything," I observed, "with your family on your back."

Gold dust, paint, and colors

I am fond of colors, including blood red, blinding yellow, and egg yolk. I am seduced by them. I entertained myself with paint cans at Les Acacias until my cranium ached. Alcohol is present in paint.

And gold powder—oh, how I cherished it. I applied it to my face and limbs. I would have bathed in a shower of gold particles if I had the ability.

Departing for New York City

I made my professional debut in Philadelphia at the Standard Theatre in a wretched revue, earning ten dollars per week—when they actually paid. I experienced hunger on the majority of evenings.

I recalled New York, money, and luxury.

I embarked on a journey to New York with only my ticket in hand. I remained in the final car, observing the rails unify into a single point.

New York was a place where males and women were at odds.

I proceeded directly to a Broadway music hall.

The director instructed me to return the following day for a week. But I was left with no money, no food, and no place to sleep. I remained in the park for three nights, shivering and being pursued by silhouettes.

The director abruptly interrupted my final attempt, stating, "No, no, no!" You are too immature. Far too unappealing. Face and physique are both unattractive. Goodbye.

However, I merely desired to perform.

I remained outside his office for more than an hour. Subsequently, I performed another strike.

"Perfect!" he exclaimed with an exhale. "Since you're so insistent, join the second company and go on tour."

We traveled from town to town for six months, occasionally performing in schoolyards.

I was the object of the males' flirtation, while the girls harbored animosity toward me.

They taunted, "You sing and act like a monkey!"

"I dance in that manner, and I will continue to do so indefinitely." I will be the one to assign you tasks in the near future.

Although they were vicious, the manager was even more so. He allocated rooms to all individuals except for me. The programs did not include my name.

One of the most prominent directors took note of me following Brooklyn.

"Please visit my office tomorrow." It is crucial.

He extended an offer of twenty dollars per week the following day.

My dressing area was a frigid corner, with water trickling from the ceiling. It was inevitable that I contracted an illness. I was confined to my bed for an entire week.

Then, I contacted my mother. "Mama, things are looking up."

She was also ill; however, she made a full recovery.

Shuffle Along and Beyond

Shuffle Along was the inaugural significant Black musical to be performed in New York. We performed for two years, specifically in 1923 and 1924. I transitioned from the second row of the chorus to the first in order to extend my arms and legs above the audience's heads.

I was employed in Washington to provide for my mother and siblings.

One day, I was the subject of an article in every newspaper.

"This is it," I concluded.

September 15, 1925. Farewell, America—Hello, Paris.

Captain W. R. D. Irvine, The Berengaria.

I observed the sea change red in the sunset as New York faded. I was not observed by anyone. What is the rationale behind this? I was a mere showgirl, a young Black girl—not even that.

The Statue of Liberty vanished. I had the support of the United States. Paris was situated ahead.

Do I possess the necessary strength? Is one sufficiently ambitious?

Nightfall occurred. Fear fled from me.

I began to sing in order to demonstrate my freedom.

"I saw the splendor of the moonlight On Honolulu Bay..."

Goodbye, New York. St. Louis, farewell. I bid you farewell, tiny girl with purple hands.

A fresh start was anticipated.

Initial Impressions of France

I had heard a great deal about the Great War, which was a dreadful event. Although I was unable to comprehend it entirely, it caused me to shed tears. I was overcome with sorrow upon witnessing individuals who were missing an arm, leg, or eye. I harbored profound pity for them. I harbored animosity toward those who caused anguish. The unfortunate were akin to my offspring, and I aspired to have them as my own. In the same way that waiters, cooks, and barmen were my siblings and young maids were my sisters.

Arrival in Cherbourg

Cold temperatures prevailed in Cherbourg. The heat in New York was unbearable, and I was only equipped with a thin parka. I contracted a severe illness. In the harbor, our enormous vessel was situated amid diminutive vessels. The city was pulsating with the sound of small trams, which were both diminutive and endearing.

There was no time to waste. We hastened from customs to the train that was already in motion at the station. I did not possess any French currency, so I presented twenty dollars to a porter.

"No, madam," he replied. "Not good."

I provided him with thirty dollars, and he accepted them.

I arrived in Paris four hours later on September 22, the same day.

Additionally, it was fortunate that it was pouring. It is believed that rain on the first day of a new city brings good fortune.

Everything appeared to be diminutive—miniscule residences, narrow streets, and diminutive footpaths. I concluded, "I will never be able to dance in this location." "Where are New York's long, straight avenues?"

Not a single word of French was familiar to me. And my American wardrobe was entirely inappropriate—simple, short dresses paired with barefoot shoes. The women's heels were high, despite the fact that the dwellings in France were small.

A Laughable Outfit

Unbeknownst to me, I dressed as a spectacle for my initial stroll through Paris. I now comprehend the reason for the laughter of others, and I am able to chuckle even more fervently than they did.

Consider the following:

Over a checkered blouse, a checkered dress with compartments is secured by two checkered straps. My cranium was adorned with a feathered hat. A camera dangling from my left buttock and a massive pair of binoculars bouncing on my right.

I am uncertain as to the reason, but Americans consistently bring a camera and binoculars when they travel abroad.

Bobby hosiery. Heels that are flat.

I set out to visit the Arc de Triomphe and Napoleon's mausoleum, all while maintaining a fashionable appearance.

2

PARIS NEWS AND VIEWS

The Initial Rehearsal—La Revue Nègre

I will always cherish the memory of our inaugural rehearsal at the Théâtre des Champs-Élysées. The Charleston was unfamiliar to them. The stage was vividly illuminated, while the room was dark. The front row was occupied by twenty individuals.

"Hello, Charleston!"

The stagehands were in awe as they observed. The fire officers were taken aback by the sound of trombones pounding in their stomachs, as they were not acclimated to the sensation.

The tiniest individuals attempted to emulate us behind the flats. Shaking their flannel-clad legs, they occasionally booted the air and each other.

The entire theater personnel convened in secrecy. Typists peered through the backdrop's openings. The fire officers laughed into their helmets. Audience members in the front row wiggled their legs. They were already ensnared by the Charleston; they had insects in their shoes.

"Yes sir, that's my baby."

The Charleston in Europe

The Charleston was initially observed by Europeans as a dance performed by Black individuals. Although they entirely altered it, they still managed to make it their own.

The Charleston was originally performed with strings of shells tinkling against the skin, producing a dry, rhythmic sound. Bananas and feathers were substituted for the shells.

Crossing your feet, thrusting out your behind, and waving your arms, you dance it with your hips, first on one side and then on the other.

Our bodies have been concealed for an excessive amount of time. Buttocks are present. What is the reason for our fear of them? Of course, some are incredibly silly, incredibly pompous, or simply mediocre—good for nothing more than lounging. However, that is not my primary concern.

Douglas and France

We were promptly welcomed by the French. I was admired by all types of individuals, as was La Revue Nègre.

I participated in a dance performance with Louis Douglas. Unfortunately, Douglas is not doing well. He was extraordinary—similar to rubber. I can still hear the clack of his soles reverberating in my ears.

He was capable of imitating any object, including a racehorse and a train, which would make a clicking sound as it moved across a black background with a small white church in the foreground. Additionally, his gums were white. He donned a mauve collar. Silence enveloped him as he danced.

Presently, he is deceased.

I believed that was the case.

However, he is alive! Someone informed me that he is currently in Marseille.

I am overjoyed to learn that.

Doug should return to the United States and establish a new Black troupe. The world is still unaware of the full extent of our capabilities.

Paris—A City That Is Unique

Have we sufficiently addressed Paris? Its rhythm, enchantment, and position in the world?

Paris is a city that embodies a combination of elegance and pandemonium, love and champagne, dance and desire. The Eiffel Tower is a pulsating beacon of light and motion. Paris adopted me, celebrated me, and provided me with everything from the very first night. In return, I harbored affection for it.

Stunning dresses, attractive women—each season reveals a new form of attractiveness. Spring will shortly become the prince of Summer. The city unfolds—sunlight at noon, golden at midnight. The Bois, afternoon tea, cabarets, music, and shopping.

Women are the essence of Paris—enigmatic and perpetually evolving. A woman who is plain and modest in the morning will reappear at night, shimmering in silk and pearls, having been transformed by the city's enchantment.

Paris is a city that I adore for its cadence and enigmas. I contemplate the women I encounter, who are hurried, beaming, and preoccupied with their thoughts. Are they on their way to work? A romantic partner? The couturier, and then the lover? Love is, after all, the most exquisite tailor.

Paris is a city of champagne, music, merriment, flowers, and frenzy at night. The streets are perpetually awake. Everywhere there is a glimmer, there is a dance. Never monotonous, never cruel—Vive Paris!

However, I am aware that the city is not solely characterized by velvet dresses and golden lighting. I am aware that there are impoverished individuals, and I also consider them.

A Residence in Every Corner of Paris

I have resided in numerous locations and communities.

From Rue Henri-Rochefort to Avenue Pierre 1er de Serbie. From Rue Fromentin to the Champs-Élysées, where I once owned a palace—a magnificent apartment with a marble swimming pool that was constructed at a significant expense. However, the luxury was not my preferred aspect. It was my infant jaguar.

Then there was Rue Henry-Monnier in Montmartre, where all the showgirls from the revue slept. We dined at La Poule du Pot for fifteen francs. I was content, despite the simplicity of the situation. I am exceedingly pleased.

The Cost of Fame: Betrayals and Lawsuits

Trouble ensued as a consequence of accomplishment.

Initially, Mrs. Dudley filed a lawsuit against me. She had been compensating me with $1,000 per month for La Revue Nègre; however, upon my departure, she requested 200,000 francs.

Then, a dance hall filed a lawsuit against me for 300,000 francs.

Then, a couturier filed a lawsuit against me; however, his claim was denied—débouté, as the French would say. Bout, dégoûté.

Of course, I will file additional lawsuits. Whenever they observe success, individuals are inclined to attempt their fortunes. That is merely the way things are.

Gifts—From Living Creatures to Jewels

I have been provided with everything.

Fire opal rings that are as large as eggs. Antique ornaments that were previously owned by a duchess. Pearls are reminiscent of dentition. Baskets of fresh blooms from Italy, their petals still damp.

Live animals—including primates, parrots, and even a pig.

A group of stuffed animals, including a cat, a rabbit, a swan, and a bear. Shoes made of gold. A dress, folded and neglected in my red handbag. Peaches of immense size. Another occasion, strawberries that were as large as my palms. Perfume contained within a glass horse. Fur upon fur upon fur.

Red-stone bracelets for my wrists, ankles, and limbs.

Sufficient.

I am currently in search of small animals that I can care for and hold.

I did, however, indulge once, purchasing a ring for 80,000 francs. What is its current location? It is probable that it is located in a neglected box.

I have never attached significant value to jewelry.

Snakeskin Automobile

The final extravagant gift of that period was a car that Monsieur Donnet presented to me. A unique model that is wholly covered in snakeskin. A wonder, a snakeskin fantasy.

On June 7, 1927, I obtained my driver's license at Porte Maillot. "Proceed, halt, and turn..."You have successfully completed the exam, Mademoiselle.

In 1936, I obtained my pilot's license.

However, I am not a sportswoman. I train differently than an automaton. I reside in a state of unpredictability and freedom.

I relocate at my discretion. I am free to extend my lips at my discretion. I am capable of crawling, running, and avoiding attention. I convey my narrative through my hands and limbs; I swim through the air, I row through the air. There you have it!

The Intriguing World of Admirers

A peculiar species is that of admirers. The pronunciation of their letters is consistent. A. B. C. D. E. F. G...Your devotee.

There are individuals who are peculiar in their appearance, style, or mannerisms. Numerous individuals lack a permanent address.

One of my acquaintances concealed himself in the Théâtre des Champs-Élysées overnight in order to observe my subsequent performance. He was unable to purchase a second ticket, and as a result, he spent the entire day and night under the seats, subsisting on chocolate bars.

Rituals and Faith

I am fortified by my faith in God.

I pray every evening before I go to bed and before I take the stage. At all times, regardless of my fatigue.

On one of my first evenings at the Folies Bergère, I knelt in my dressing room, hands clasped, and head bowed, completely naked. I was sorrowful; however, I reserve specific sorrows for my prayers.

The stage manager entered without knocking.

I gazed at him. He discreetly exited, closing the door behind him.

I concluded my supplication.

Parisian performance

I participated in a dance at the residence of Monsieur Dreyfus. I participated in the Bal des Petits Lits Blancs, a charity gala held at the Opéra, where I danced in the presence of 40,000 golden lanterns.

Gold and white. Silver and white.

I danced on the Silver Bridge amidst a multitude of faces, my hands fluttering beneath me. Monsieur Poincaré was seated in a diminutive box, his sparse gray beard discernible from a distance. I struck my leg against his eyeline. He chuckled.

A Christmas Dream

In 1926, I purchased a Christmas tree for the children of Parisian police officers. A fir tree adorned with miniature candles, glass eggs, wafers, and toys.

I had always aspired to be a youthful, Black Mother Christmas.

My greatest pleasure was the applause emanating from those diminutive hands.

However, I was incensed when I observed children who were not invited—rich children who were outfitted in high-quality shoes and were indifferent to my gifts. Snobs.

I will never be able to forgive those who permitted them to enter.

Next time, I will execute the task independently.

I will purchase toys and treats.

I will independently visit the facilities.

I will distribute them to the children with melancholy expressions.

I am able to ignore my own childhood as a result of these moments.

Assist me in forgetting the snow that fell in St. Louis.

Forget the frigid residences of Black families.

Ignore Bernard Street, where we were so impoverished.

A Lucky Charm and a Dictionary

I now possess the compendium I have always desired—a seven-volume set that is replete with illustrations. However, I never examine the interior; I lack the leisure. Rather, I hold each volume in my palms and chuckle. Ultimately, the weight of words is not that significant.

For what reason?

Due to my preference for fairy tales, which are among the most charming novels. Presently, I am engaged in the perusing of Contes Dorés. Have you ever heard the tale of the man who had an affinity for insects? He spent his life walking on his hands, with his legs suspended in the air, in order to prevent them from being crushed. The golden, silver, and shimmering forms of the tiny barrels, which were poised on needle-thin legs, were lined up and prepared to sting. He admired their beauty.

The Mysteries of the Rabbit's Foot

I have been extremely fortunate.

Dancers are observed to be radiant under the spotlights; however, what transpires after the curtain has been drawn? Out of the thousands of individuals who occupy the stage, only one in a million is recognized as a celebrity. The remainder perish prematurely.

I am well-versed in this matter. Additionally, I am entirely dependent on my rabbit's foot.

One evening, while I was still performing at 64th Street, a peculiar little man appeared at the door of my dressing room. He was characterized by a drooping shoulder, bulging eyes, and brilliant ginger hair.

"I have relocated from South Carolina," he declared. "I encountered a family member of yours." This gift was sent to you by him; please ensure its safety. It will bring you excellent fortune.

He presented me with a rabbit's foot.

I was dissatisfied at the time. I performed all the appropriate superstitions, such as gazing over my left shoulder at the new moon and shaking a coin in my right palm, but fortune had not yet found me.

Nevertheless, I obtained the rabbit's foot.

I was once again met by the same diminutive individual the following evening.

"You must never lose it," he cautioned. "It is your most valuable asset." I assure you that you will forfeit everything if you do.

Then, he clicked his tongue and vanished into the wings.

I deposited the rabbit's foot in my powder box that evening. I placed it beneath my pillow while I slept.

I half anticipated his return the following evening. Rather, a tall, slender man was stationed at my entrance.

He presented me with an envelope and inquired, "Are you Mademoiselle Baker?"

A letter was enclosed, which read, "Please visit me to discuss employment opportunities."

I fled. I was unable to exhale. I arrived and tapped.

"Enter." Would you be interested in dancing at the newly established Plantation Club on Broadway? Attached is your contract.

My departure was marked by mirth. I proceeded to dance throughout the entire length of the street. For an hour, I kissed the foot of my rabbit.

I was en route to Paris six months later.

Rabbit's Foot Loss

An evening at the Théâtre des Champs-Élysées, I was unable to locate my rabbit's foot.

I conducted an exhaustive inspection of my hotel room, my bedroom, and the backstage area. Disappeared.

However, I did observe something peculiar. Josie Smith, an additional showgirl, had recently executed an agreement with a London-based music hall.

Suspicion was in my mind.

One day, I entered Josie's dressing room, where she was employing my rabbit's foot as a particle for her rice powder.

I was aware of it!

I slept peacefully that night with my dear rabbit's foot tucked beneath my pillow, despite the fact that we had a disagreement.

I attended the races at Longchamp a few days later. It was the Prix de l'Arc de Triomphe.

I considered placing a wager. "Since I have my rabbit's foot again."

I bet on two horses. I was awarded 400,000 francs.

That is my concealment: a rabbit's foot.

Motto of Josephine

Josephine Baker frequently asserts, "The activities that I derive pleasure from are the culmination of my existence."

That is her credo.

She consistently demonstrates this.

The Absent Star

The theater was entirely filled. Opera glasses in hand, the audience awaited. The orchestra performed. However, where was Josephine?

The stage manager was in a state of despair. He conducted an examination of the dressing rooms and the stairwells. She is nowhere to be found.

The director became pallid. A vehicle was dispatched to Josephine's residence. Nothing.

The running order was altered upon returning to the theater. An additional march was performed by the orchestra. Catastrophe.

What was her location?

In conjunction with the concierge.

She had arrived early that evening and in passing by the concierge's chamber, she detected a delectable aroma.

She exclaimed, "What an extraordinary soup!"

Josephine requested a sample. Subsequently, she consumed the entire saucepan, followed by a Camembert, and requested champagne.

Concurrently, the theater was in a state of disorder.

Ultimately, she dashed backstage, ascended the stairs in a flurry, stripped, donned her skimpy red costume, and ascended the stage.

She extended her arms in response to the ovation.

"What a delicious soup!"

The Lobster Incident

Another night, another absent Josephine.

No one was present at the concierge's desk. There was no one in the stairwells. The door to her dressing room was secured.

The director, who was now in a state of agitation, directed that it be opened.

She was reclining on the floor, unclothed, with a langouste in one hand and a pair of scissors in the other, contently dissecting it.

She jumped to her feet, scarcely finished chewing, and dashed to the stage.

The audience erupted in applause.

Ultimately, it had been an exceptional langouste.

A Theater Filled with Rabbits

Rabbits are currently housed in Josephine Baker's dressing area.

A complaint has been submitted by the theater director.

It is not specifically about the rabbits.

But regarding the rodent droppings.

Additionally, the aroma.

3

FIRST TOUR OF THE OLD AND NEW WORLDS

Twenty-five countries, two years

from 1928 to 1930, I traveled to twenty-five countries in Europe and North America.

The Netherlands

We traversed a vast bridge that appeared to be kilometers in length, traversing yellow, sluggish water that was as still as if it were slumber. The Netherlands was situated on the opposite shore.

Canals supplanted roads in the fields, yet they were imperceptible to the naked eye. It appeared as though boats were gliding on air, weightless and unhurried.

At the following venue, I executed my

Rotterdam's Grand Theater

The Scala Theatre in The Hague

Scheveningen's Palais de Danse

Amsterdam's Concertgebouw

Monsieur Sauvage, success is not about admiration or acclaim. It is about the love that is invested in the task. However, being a curiosity was an unappreciated endeavor. Performances were not the sole requirement of my contracts. I was required to perform in cabarets after each performance, as I did at my club in Montmartre. I was responsible for making grand ladies dance in their stiff gowns and flattering elderly gentlemen. People required entertainment, and they were under the impression that I appreciated it as well. Occasionally, I did. However, their expectations were not realized.

1928 was the year in which it all began in the Netherlands.

I was cordially welcomed at the Tuschinski cabaret. The Dutch are usually serious and rosy, and they consume well. They rarely smile, but when they do, it is sincere. They are able to speak three or four languages with ease.

My name was soon recognized throughout the nation.

At one time, in a tranquil small town, individuals approached me on the street, grabbed my sleeve, and requested that I perform. I performed a dance, and they rose in enthusiastic applause. A woman observed the event while holding an infant in her arms. I reached for the infant, intending to rock and hold him. Perhaps even engage in a dance with him. However, the mother became tense, glared, and grabbed him away.

She rescued her infant from the savage.

Even in the Netherlands and other countries, there were individuals who would have been delighted to provide me with pulverized glass. They discussed the animalistic fervor of primitive instincts. Always the same prejudices, disguised in different language.

However, Paris is currently my wilderness. I adore it with all my heart; it is as intoxicating as wine, despite the fact that I am unable to consume it, as it immediately affects my mind. For two years, I labored diligently abroad in order to return to Paris. Upon my return, Paris greeted me with a round of ovation.

Rotterdam, Amsterdam, and The Hague

The Hague was characterized by red bricks, bicycles, and police officers who wore white gloves, resembling Negro comedians in revue performances.

Rotterdam and Amsterdam—energized, vibrant, and brimming with colors. Shifting and flashing in every hue, much like a kaleidoscope. The Dutch have a fondness for vibrant colors, such as intense reds and yellows.

The country of water, sand, and fir trees was my home for a month, from August to September 1928. Also, I developed an affection for it.

True affection for a nation necessitates dressing in accordance with its populace.

Therefore, I donned a full-length dress, a Dutch headpiece, and wooden clogs. In yellow clogs, I executed the Charleston. I transported milk in iron churns. Pepito laughed until he was unable to breathe.

I do not smoke; however, if I were to do so, I would have adopted a clay pipe, as the spouses of fishermen do.

In Scheveningen, women are adorned with gold antennas on their bonnets, which vibrate as they stride, evoking an exquisite and peculiar appearance reminiscent of insects.

The sea in that location is distinct from all other seas. Always gray, always wrinkled, and never sleek or shiny. However, a picturesque avenue of trees connects The Hague to Scheveningen Beach, where brass musicians dazzle in the sunlight.

I am of the opinion that my performances were successful, as they requested my return.

Ah, and the chocolate, the tulips, and the cheeses—it was spectacular.

Danish, Swedish, and Norwegian

"Kiss my nose, Monsieur Sauvage, and please…don't be upset with me anymore."

Josephine tilts her head with a shoulder movement that resembles a machine.

"If the borders appear blurry in my memory, it is due to my lack of interest in them." Why is it necessary for yesterday to influence the present? However, if you are adamant, Denmark, Sweden, and Norway are viable options.

The three most democratic nations.

I appreciate courtesy.

One evening, while I was performing in Central Europe—or perhaps it was not even Europe—I observed a fellow in the front row reading a newspaper.

He was present the following evening, concealing himself behind his paper.

In the third night, I peered through the drapery. He was present, with a newspaper in his hand.

I ascended the stage on tiptoe, bowed toward the conductor, and requested that the music cease.

"Mr. Conductor, are you unable to perceive?" For the past three days, this individual has been endeavoring to read.

I then turned to the man and smiled sweetly:

"I apologize, sir, but I comprehended your message on the initial occasion." "Now, would you object?"

Copenhagen, Oslo, Stockholm, and Gothenburg—Forty-five days from June to August 1928.

Copenhagen: Dagmar Theater, followed by late-night performances at the Adlon club.

Stockholm: The Winter Garden at the Grand Hôtel, followed by the Oscar Theater.

Oslo: First, a theater performance, followed by a cabaret show.

Consistently the same configuration.

They were the most impeccably maintained nations I had ever encountered.

At first, I was daunted by its cleanliness.

I performed for a regal family in Copenhagen. I entertained the monarch in Stockholm. However, when you inquire about his appearance, I would be unable to provide you with an answer. I am the only one in sight when I dance, not even a monarch.

A crowd congregated beneath the window of my hotel in Copenhagen. I threw photographs to them on an impulse.

I have never observed such a large number of straw headwear that have been crushed.

Although the spectacle caused me to chuckle, I was profoundly moved.

Every evening in Oslo, two attractive police officers on horseback escorted me from the theater to my hotel. Not only was it flattering, but it was also humiliating. Individuals gazed at one another. Therefore, in order to alleviate the situation, I engaged in lighthearted banter with the officers, thereby ensuring that all individuals were aware that I had not been apprehended.

I had six detectives on foot in Stockholm. They saluted me in the manner of a general. The size of their eyes required me to crane my neck in order to gaze upon them. In Sweden, I experienced an overwhelming sense of insignificance.

Beneath the Midnight Sun

The sun is a comedian in that location.

It is raining. Suddenly, the sun emerges. Then, it showers once more. Oh, my goodness!

In contrast, the midnight sun is an entirely different phenomenon. It is daylight when you enter the theater. You depart; although it is still daylight, it is now night.

I engaged in fishing under the peculiar sun. The fjord was tranquil, and the air was fresh. However, an abrupt gust of wind pierced the warmth like a blade of ice.

In order to maintain my body temperature, I was placed beneath a sunshade. The air was permeated by the aroma of tallow, fish, tar, and aged leather. I experienced nausea.

Nevertheless, the sea itself served as a source of tranquility for me. Its cadence against the boat's hull was steady and calming. The sound of its whisper soothed me to slumber.

I will always cherish the experience of fishing in the fjords.

In Copenhagen, each residence is equipped with a mast, similar to that of a ship. They raise their flags every Sunday.

Stockholm, a city encircled by water and islands, is a city of banners.

I encountered Einar Lundborg, the aviator who had recently rescued General Nobile, at that location. He stopped by my dressing room to extend his greetings. I was rendered speechless—what could a dancer possibly convey to a hero?

I maintain my silence when I encounter an individual whom I respect.

However, it brought me immense joy.

Successfully Conquering Stockholm

Stockholm was a challenging city to dominate.

A city that is characterized by sophistication. Its inhabitants were apprehensive toward me and my banana belt.

Newspapers engaged in discussions.

Monsieur Berman, a journalist, defended me:

"What is the percentage of white individuals in this room who have a black heart?" This is a discussion of art, not nudity. "Will Stockholm reject an individual who has conquered Paris?"

I will refrain from reiterating the remainder. Sweden exceeded its bounds. And perhaps I did as well.

However, they ultimately comprehended. One of the most heartfelt greetings I have encountered was theirs. My performances were fully attended by the Swedish Academy.

They referred to me as "the angel of the Negro race" during my time there.

It is excessive. I am not a divinity. It causes me considerable embarrassment to reiterate it.

However, wasn't it a generous gesture on their part?

White lands with crystalline lakes, surrounded by blue mountains—these are Sweden and Norway.

Denmark is level and illuminated.

Scandinavia—where they have a fondness for France and Paris.

Oh, and I nearly overlooked that! There, they consume nutritious meals. An abundance of cream. Additionally, each individual is exceedingly well-informed.

Awakening of a Traveler

Every new country, regardless of our preferences, alters us. It sharpens our vision, acclimates our ears to unfamiliar melodies, and introduces us to spirits that we had previously only observed through distorted reflections. The most subtle truths—the fragile, untranslatable ones—can only be comprehended through personal experience.

Monsieur Sauvage, that is the explanation I am attempting to provide. I am profoundly affected by it; however, I am unable to articulate it. I would be required to either chant or dance to it.

A new country is comparable to a new melody. It has evolved into a dance that I aspire to master by the time I depart.

I have acquired numerous aliases during my travels, including Giuseppina, La Bakerova, Koséfina, Phifine, and Pepel, as they referred to me in Vienna. What is the reason for Pepel? I was previously unaware that compassion necessitates no explanation.

I gained a deeper understanding of France with each excursion. Additionally, Paris—oh, Paris!—Paris serves as the West's guiding light. Apex.

Dancing for Princesses

I nearly neglected to inform you that the King of Denmark requested that I perform a performance for the young princesses during a visit to Copenhagen one afternoon.

They sat in a circle on velvet cushions, applauding and giggling as I moved. They were pretty, blonde, and rosy-cheeked. However, I was more content than they were.

Since I believe that all young males are kings and all young girls are princesses. The purest expression of royalty is a child's wonder.

Monsieur Sauvage, wouldn't you concur?

Any infant can be transformed into a prince through a tantrum.

I have always been captivated by the concept of monarchs. I would relish the opportunity to peruse a history of kings that is intended for youth, a history that is universally applicable.

However, I am merely a performer. A performer. I have dedicated my existence to the stage.

I was unable to accept the gift of a child. Not yet.

This is the source of my sorrow.

It is possible that this is the reason for my intense affection for baby creatures.

I will recount the tales of all of my animals if you desire at some point.

The illegal importation of dogs into Sweden

On the subject of wildlife...

Sweden has a regulation that prohibits the presence of canines. It is strictly prohibited.

However, I was accompanied by two dogs when I departed from Denmark: Phyllis and her spouse, a plump, round creature that was as large as a coconut.

Captain of the vessel maintained his resolve:

"Madame, you cannot bring dogs into Sweden."

"Captain," I replied, "I have never abandoned anyone, and I certainly will not begin with my dogs." I will not enter Sweden if they are unable to.

Panic. The impresario became pallid. Telegrams were transmitted to the Swedish Ministers of Agriculture and Hygiene—a remarkable feat. Ministers! For my pets!

Long hours passed as cables traversed the ocean. Permission was ultimately granted.

Phyllis and her husband were granted official passports, provided that they refrain from leaving my hotel room.

Naturally, I refrained from complying.

Phyllis was expecting a child. She required exposure to pure air. I would sneak out with her for a covert walk every morning before dawn.

Then, one day, she gave birth.

I was apprehended by a police officer while walking her spouse that morning. I sprinted back to my room before he could halt me, only for the pups to begin barking.

The door was knocked on.

"Are your dogs declared?"

"Yes, sir."

"Admitted?"

"Yes, sir."

"How many?"

"Two, sir."

"And those?" he inquired, pointing to Phyllis's infants, which were still no larger than plums.

"Oh, those?" I grinned. "They are barely dogs, sir." In the process of acquiring the necessary skills. You would not wish for me to return them to their original location, would you?

The police officer was not delighted.

The personnel of the hotel were subjected to questioning. The director was summoned. The minister of agriculture was nearly roused from his slumber.

Phyllis's condition was not favorable.

Subsequently, I experienced an abundance of mirth.

Budapest to Bucharest—Romania

I was employed as a symbol in Central Europe and later in South America, where I was compelled to choose between opposing factions.

I did not request it.

However, politicians transform everything into a political issue, don't they?

The traditional Catholic organizations, incensed by my liberation, pursued me from city to city and from station to stage. Fights ensued. The streets were invaded by police officers wielding swords. I observed males sprinting past me, holding revolvers.

Even in Vienna—Vienna! A sister metropolis to Paris! They issued a warning to the devout by ringing the church bells at full peal:

"Josephine Baker, the demon of immorality, has arrived!"

Chaos prevailed throughout Central Europe on my visit.

Fear was observed by me.

And I will never forget that certain leaders—men who should have known better—found it imperative to oppose a dancer.

Yet, I continued to offer my petitions each evening, despite all of this.

Nor did it prevent me from harboring affection for France; rather, I now harbored a more mature affection for her.

Bucharest, Romania

Romania!

France is highly esteemed by Romanians. Therefore, it was only natural that I held them in high regard.

June 1928, Bucharest.

The Eforia Theater.

Only the most affluent individuals in Bucharest possess automobiles.

But the coachmen—ah!—they are something altogether different.

Men who are soft-spoken and are clothed in the style of Russian nobility, with long embroidered sleeves and tall hats.

Furthermore, they were all eunkuchs.

The Sights and Aromas of Romania

You encountered cows, pigs, and poultry in the streets—what an unpleasant odor!

In the lodgings, there are fleas and insects with an excessive number of legs.

However, the fruits!

The most delicious and largest I had ever encountered.

Monsieur Tănase and His Legendary Nose

Ah, but I must inform you about Monsieur Tănase.

The most renowned individual in Romania.

Not because he was an exceptional impresario, which he was.

It was not due to his exceptional talent as a performer (although he was).

However, this is due to his appearance.

The enormity, expressiveness, and impossibility of the ridge were nearly tragic.

Each infant of Tănase was endowed with a nose that was equivalent to three noses.

You would be able to identify them immediately.

Nevertheless, they were obedient, consistently adhering to their father like devoted puppies.

Not that there was ever any risk of losing sight of him!

Dancing in the Rain

I would now like to introduce you to my final evening at the Cărăbuș Theater.

An outdoor theater.

Black clouds approached.

The temperature is extremely high. The thunderbolt!

Monsieur Tănase was in full panic.

For what reason?

He would be required to refund the entire audience if the rain arrived before the show was midway through.

The entire audience had been packed into a 1,700-seat venue, with 3,000 individuals in attendance.

Thunder rumbled.

After that, there was a loud bang.

The conductor's head was struck by the initial descent.

The orchestra increased its speed.

We were compelled to outpace the tempest.

I ascended to take the stage.

The heavens collapsed.

Umbrellas appeared in a similar manner to fungi.

Women elevated their skirts above their shoulders.

I continued to dance while grabbing an umbrella.

The orchestra performed in the presence of an ocean of umbrellas.

The horns gurgled with water.

My banana girdle was saturated. The bananas, which were damp, fell onto the stage with a thud.

The audience erupted in applause.

As a wet chicken, my plumage clung to my body as I was drenched.

However, I proceeded to perform.

And the orchestra performed.

We emerged victorious.

That was quite a tempest! What a night! What an audience!

"That, Monsieur Sauvage, was Romania."

Should we proceed to Prague at this time?

The Lucerna Theater—A Battle Against the Orchestra Lucerna was struck by a disaster.

The vast stage of one of Europe's largest underground theaters rendered performers appear diminutive, their voices being absorbed by the shear enormity of the space. It accommodated eight thousand individuals that evening.

I recalled a chilling fact as I stood under the lights: the massive conduit that supplied Prague's water ran just above the theater. Within minutes, we could all be submerged by a single fissure or leak. I briefly examined the ceiling. No water was dripped, and no damp areas were disseminated.

I dismissed the notion.

The performance commenced.

Initially, I was apprehensive, and my voice seemed to float into the ether. Then the initial surges of applause reached me. Dispersed, yet encouraging. Fire from a loose cannon.

Next, the orchestra initiated my dance music.

I concluded, "The worst is behind us." "I'm saved."

I traversed the stage from right to left, ensuring that I covered every inch. However, the orchestra rapidly increased its pace. I glanced at the conductor, who appeared unconcerned, his pallid hands flickering like ghostly wings, swatting at invisible notes.

More rapidly. And more rapidly.

I increased the intensity of my dancing in order to maintain pace, stamping my foot in protest as I approached the pit. Nothing. Lost in the music, his pupils were wide and his arms were moving frantically.

"Too fast, too fast!" I yelled.

My words dissipated amid the disorder.

The frenzy seized control. My movements were no longer my own, as I spun erratically.

Suddenly, there was a slip. The stage was struck with force by me. My side was racked with agony as my arm was abrasively scraped against the floor. However, I immediately rose to my feet.

Applause erupted from the audience. They believed that it was an integral component of the legislation.

I shouted once more, "Trop vite!" However, the conductor, who was either incompetent or deranged, incited the musicians to engage in a final, frantic run.

I landed on my knees, allowing blood to seep down my legs and into my stockings. You are done if you cease at this moment.

Consequently, I engaged in a dance.

I danced with the intensity of a demon, propelled by exhaustion and rage. I outlasted them by leaping, spinning, and running.

Eventually, the conductor's arm dipped. The music abruptly ceased.

Lucerna, this immense cavern of faces, was obscured in my vision. The audience erupted in a deep, reverberating clamor.

Then, "blackness."

I was rendered unconscious.

My arms were draped around myself as blood seeped into the rug as they carried me to my dressing room, my body drained.

Vienna—A City of Beauty and Controversy

Vienna. The sister metropolis of Paris. A location that is characterized by waltzes, romance, and music.

Additionally, it was a city that was at conflict with me.

A campaign against me had been initiated prior to my arrival.

Monsieur Jerzabek, a politician, determined to elevate me to the status of a symbol, thereby endangering Austria's morality. He carried his crusade all the way to Parliament, warning that I symbolized the moral decay that was hovering over the country.

Father Frey, a Jesuit priest, then came to the pulpit and declared that I was the embodiment of Lust.

Vienna anticipated the arrival of a demon, rather than a performer.

The Warning and the Church Bells

The city's church bells tolled in warning as my train approached, rather than in celebration.

The streets were inundated with pamphlets:

"Allow this woman to be punished." She is the embodiment of immorality.

Nevertheless, thousands of individuals visited me, despite the outrage.

For what reason? Viennese women are the least envious in the world, as they are elegant, delicate, and loving, and Viennese men are charming.

The twin wonders of Europe are Parisian and Viennese ladies.

Nevertheless, I was subjected to an escort by the authorities that was unlike anything I had ever encountered. My every movement was monitored by an armada of officers who were as rigid as butlers.

Vienna's Protests: The Reality

Indeed, there were demonstrations.

Yes, there was rage.

However, was it truly about me?

It was a period of crisis. Unemployment was elevated. Tickets were exceedingly costly.

It is possible that the rioters outside the theater were not enraged by Josephine Baker, but rather by the impossible luxury that was on display. Models were parading gowns worth twenty-five thousand francs, while hungry men stood outside, empty-handed.

Was their fury unwarranted?

However, I had not yet established the prices.

The fashion display had not been staged by me.

I have only come to perform.

Additionally, I do not regard the dollar as a deity.

And Vienna Listens—The Church Condemns Me

Father Frey assumed the pulpit at St. Paul's, which is situated directly across from my theater, the night prior to my début.

The church was packed with individuals who were anticipating his denunciation of me.

Rather, he portrayed me as the embodiment of Europe's transgressions, speaking with a melancholy tone.

"Josephine Baker is not the cause of our corruption," he asserted. "She is merely its reflection."

What a privilege. All of Europe's crimes are placed at my feet.

That evening, my theater was filled with the same individuals who had previously listened to him.

They had arrived to witness the devil's oration.

My Response to Vienna

I entered the platform.

The audience was eerily silent.

There will be no jeers. Protests are prohibited.

Silence.

Then, I began to sing.

Not a seductive number. It was not the chaotic rhythms they anticipated.

However, an old slave song—a Negro spiritual:

"Sleep, my poor baby…"

An ode to anguish.

A composition that expresses hopelessness.

A hymn from a time when men and women of my ethnicity were only useful for dying in fields, where they were labored to death by the most Christian of masters.

The theater's walls trembled with acclaim as soon as I concluded.

I danced in the same manner as I have always done, not to provoke or defy.

I danced to demonstrate the sufficiency of life, to demonstrate freedom, and to express pleasure.

Life is good!

Monsieur Sauvage, the Black Demon prays each evening.

Regardless of her level of fatigue, she prays upon her return home.

Ensure that you record that information.

Vienna—A City That Chose to Love Me

By this time, the Austrians had embraced me. In the most eccentric individual in Central Europe, Count Sternberg, I discovered an unexpected ally. He was a relic of old nobility, deprived of his title by revolution, and a fearless defender of mine. He was a devout Catholic. The text on his business card was as follows:

"Charlemagne bestowed upon me a title." It was stolen from me by the son of a blacksmith.

He arrived in Vienna at the same time as I did, prepared to deliver a lecture on the League of Nations and, later that evening, a speech about me.

The Vienna elite convened, wearing dark suits and low-necklines. Eccentricity has historically been considered scandalous by the global community; however, it has become increasingly fashionable in recent years.

The audience was taken aback when Count Sternberg took the stage and delivered remarks that caused a gasp:

"The League of Nations is a club for giant stomachs and minuscule brains."

"If Christ returned, Europeans and Americans would unite to nail him to a cross of pure gold."

Afterward, he discussed me:

"White individuals are incapable of dancing." If you are in search of the authentic art of dance, travel to Asia or Africa. From expressions of pleasure and sorrow to movements that captivate gods and demons, only colored people have preserved its sacred essence.

"The nude female form has consistently represented the pinnacle of human art." However, the clerics who condemn Josephine Baker fail to acknowledge the numerous nude figures that adorn the Sistine Chapel.

"The Vatican silently condemns tormented Black priests while obsessing over a woman who dances."

"The pinnacle of female beauty is achieved through dance." The earliest Christians in Arabia and Palestine once performed the belly dance. Did this "damned" ritual impede the Copts from being the most devoted Catholics?

Prejudices were fractured by his remarks. I was assured of my victory in Vienna. I capitalized on the absence of church bells that tolled in dissent as I traversed the streets.

Accompanied by my Parisian jazz ensemble, I danced at the Wolf's Pavilion, Vienna's most fashionable cabaret, each evening. By day, I traversed the city, taking in the vibrant cafés, St. Stephen's Cathedral, Schönbrunn's gardens, and, of course, the renowned Wiener Schnitzel.

The unadulterated bliss of Viennese coffee with whipped cream, or Schlagsahne. This coffee was so cherished that an opera was composed in its honor.

Vienna was the location.

Hungary—Between Love and Chaos

An disconcerting sight greeted me at the Budapest station:

A series of film cameras.

A line of soldiers with their weapons drawn.

Police officers standing in a lineup, each with a firearm.

Budapest was my destination on two separate occasions, in 1928 and 1929. In order to circumvent controversy and the unwanted presence of weapons, I traveled in covert on the second occasion. However, Budapest remains one of my most memorable experiences.

I genuinely believed that the Danube could be azure in this location.

Budapest, the Queen of the Danube, unfurled beneath the wings of a magnificent bronze eagle perched on a precipitous cliff. Buda and Pest, each side equally picturesque, are immersed in history. I was, as usual, enthusiastic about acquiring knowledge.

Violins and Romance: The Sound of Hungary

Budapest may be the most romantic metropolis in Europe. In order to comprehend it entirely, it is necessary to listen to its violins.

At sunset, the golden Danube, with its majestic bridges, appears to trail behind the sun like a shimmering train, as Hungarian violins quiver softly yet intensely.

No city greeted me with more enthusiasm—or more resistance.

Hungary's Admiration and Abhorrence of Josephine Baker

Parliament debated my presence on three separate occasions prior to my arrival.

They referred to me as the Black Demon, as they had done in Vienna.

In order to obtain entry, I was required to perform privately for a government censorship board. My conduct was meticulously observed by the minister in command.

Subsequently, he demonstrated his approval.

He even requested an encore.

"You are overdressed," he observed.

Consequently, I readily explored Budapest with their consent.

This is a city of baths, with Gellért Hill, its caverns, and its belt of hot springs. Budapest's Champs-Élysées, also known as Andrássy út. The Orpheum Theater, where I performed, was situated at the intersection of Elizabeth Boulevard. The steps of the theater were fringed with peasant women who were selling intricate, handcrafted embroidery. What is the reason for the lack of widespread adoption of Hungarian embroidery?

The Ammonia Bomb—Dancing Through Danger

The Orpheum was entirely filled. I initiated my performance, becoming engrossed in the cadence. Then, an unusual disturbance ensued.

I raised my head.

A man threw an object into the throng while leaning over the gallery.

An explosive device.

My epidermis was pricked for an infinite amount of time. I closed my eyes.

A resounding crash.

Next, there was a period of silence.

It was not an explosive; rather, it was an ammonia device. However, a woman in the audience was still burnt.

I concluded, "Hungarians are truly extravagant."

I continued to dance.

Budapest's Magic—Despite It All On terraces with panoramic views of the Danube, Hungarian violins were played.

A tragic tale was told by the city's oldest bridge, which was defended by two massive stone lions. The sculptor was so disheartened that he flung himself into the river upon discovering that his lions lacked tongues. His body drifted ashore on Margaret Island, which is known for its rose gardens.

The Hungarian Parliament, the largest in Europe, was situated across the Danube. The historic Buda Castle and white church spires are situated on one side, while the elegant streets of Pest are situated on the other. Violins, bathhouses, and the lively bustle of life are present in every location.

I was reminded of the Spaniards by the late brunches, paprika-laced dishes, and unwavering passion for music that Hungarians possessed.

The chicken with paprika is exceptional.

Crepes that are accompanied by jam or hazelnuts are even more delightful.

A violin performing in the background is indispensable.

However, my initial visit was accompanied by a surge of prudence. The bomb, the protests, the weeping...a theater filled with individuals, who were observing me through their weeping.

The second visit was distinguished from the first.

I entered the stage carrying a bouquet of Hungary's national hues. Mistinguett, the French icon, was seated in the audience. I tossed my bouquet into the crowd and dedicated my performance to France.

This time, I was greeted with a resounding round of acclaim.

Spain—A Land of Dreams

Combs that are as tall as skyscrapers, castanets, citrus trees, penitents in pointed hoods, wrought-iron balconies, bullfights, and flamenco...

Spain is the country in question.

I anticipated a golden sun and blooms adorning balconies upon my arrival in Madrid. Rather, I discovered snow. It was disappointing, but it is forgivable, as it evaporated within a day.

Spain was a world apart, a village that was unaffected by time, yet was alive with color, music, and life.

Valencia's rice, which was prepared with poultry, shrimp, mussels, and peppers, was unparalleled.

They informed me that Barcelona is a city that is distinct from Spain. It was Carnival, and I sang in Catalan. The streets were adorned with confetti, and streamers entwined around me like ribbons of delight.

I completed my performance in the small municipality of Huesca and then bowed.

And then, a tempest ensued.

Hats, coats, handkerchiefs, ties, suspenders, jackets, and shoes were flung onto the stage in wild enthusiasm, rather than applause.

I was on the brink of weeping, as I was feeling overpowered.

I had made every effort to the best of my ability.

However, at that precise instant, I was uncertain whether to laugh or flee after being mistaken for a toro.

A Spectacle of Tradition—Seville

Upon exiting the train, I was confronted with a vision that astonished me: aisles of figures in pointed hoods, their torches flickering during the night. The penitents, who were dressed in elaborate costumes, marched through the streets during Holy Week, singing to the accompaniment of the strumming of guitars while carrying gilded crosses. The ambiance was both solemn and captivating.

Seville is the Spain of legend, where women elegantly drape themselves in scintillating mantillas and the air is infused with passion. In the city, there was no space due to the Ibero-American Exposition, which had attracted throngs from all over during my visit. I was able to locate a cot with a family that was impoverished; however, it was too short for me. During those eight nights, I was unable to sleep, as I was captivated by the vivacious hum of Seville by the Guadalquivir.

There were spiders, centipedes, and ladybugs that inhabited the chamber, and they were all marching along the ceiling. Ultimately, I relinquished control, allowing my feet to suspend from the bed and allowing the small creatures to proceed. I would then venture out to explore the city, following the gentle guitar strums and the jingling keys of the serenos, the night watchmen.

A Petition Against Me—Pamplona

I had recently paid forty pesetas in Seville to attend a religious event, and the church was situated directly across from the theater. Surely, I was entitled to some consideration. However, the Catholic Mothers Association initiated a petition against me that was both aggressive and filled with outrage.

Fortunately, they were unable to persuade the mayor. I had danced in Madrid without divine punishment or royal censure, so why not here? The show continued, and I was amused when a few heavy hats were hurled at me, which I caught in midair like discuses.

Valladolid—the City of the Ancient Books

The library that differentiates it from all others is situated in the historic capital. I was presented with manuscripts that were bound in leather and adorned with gemstones and ivory. Red capital letters continued to bleed across the pages of certain volumes, which were so large that they could have been used as dining tables.

A Tour of the Music and Dance of Spain

There are numerous communities, including Málaga, San Sebastián, Oviedo, Santander, Logroño, and Gijón, whose names are as easily pronounced as castanets.

They performed the jota for me in Zaragoza—a mesmerizing and rhythmic performance. I yearned to be a part of the circle of hands that were applauding.

I witnessed a comedy that was choreographed in the same manner as a ballet in Valencia, the metropolis of orange trees. There, I consumed rice, which remains a vivid memory in my visions, as well as paella. However, I will refrain from discussing it further; I have already waxed poetic about that rice.

Córdoba, Córdoba, Córdoba—the mere mention of the name evokes images of gardens, palaces, courtyards with bulging earthenware jars, and small, round trees. It is Spain in its most pristine state.

Next, there was Granada—a realm characterized by the enchanting Alhambra, cypress-lined paths, oleander, and citrus trees. I marveled at the Moorish splendor of the palace as I strolled through fragrant gardens, surrounded by fountains, roses, and jasmine.

However, the Gypsies, who were impoverished, were present in addition to the Generalife's grandeur. Living in earthen homes, they smoked incessantly, their voices hushed yet resonant with emotion, and sang love songs as copper was beaten in cadence from morning to twilight.

Spain—A Delirious Joyride

Spain is a nation that is perpetually in motion, its fervor unwavering.

Although I may have performed in each city, this tour was a journey of affection for me.

Germany—A Nation of Contradictions

After spending my early years in France, Germany was the first European country I visited. They extended a cordial welcome to me, and they even extended me contracts, including one from the renowned theater director Max Reinhardt. It is possible that I would have pursued an acting career in Germany had I accepted in 1926. However, my reputation belonged to Paris.

Monsieur Sauvage, you expressed your admiration for Germany, including its underground brasseries, poets, and remarkable machinery. However, are you able to comprehend the German mind? I am unable to.

Berlin is one hundred times more illuminated at night than Paris, and Germany is a nation that values order and illumination. However, the specter of suicide persists in this land of efficiency and comfort. I was introduced to that apparition during my second visit. I greeted it and quaffed a drink.

A Scandal and a Triumph—Berlin

A frenzy, Berlin was a place of lunacy. I was greeted with acclaim during my initial performance.

The musicians in one dance hall ceased to perform upon my arrival. They stood, bowed, and resumed their activities.

I received a greater number of love letters, flowers, and presents in Berlin than in any other location.

Max Reinhardt approached me with a contract in his hand:

"Sign with me, stay for three years at the Deutsches Theater, and you'll be the biggest star in Europe."

However, my affection was bound to the Folies Bergère. I had already made my commitment.

The crowd at a grand costume ball was so densely crowded that it was impossible to move, with men and women crammed together like sardines. The room was crowded with black individuals, an uncommon occurrence in Berlin. I served as a member of the judging jury for a contest to determine the most stylish woman.

There was an oddly French quality to Berlin—a city that was grand, spotless, and orderly.

I was hailed as the embodiment of German Expressionism by German newspapers and publications.

"Alles für Josephine!"

They found it humorous. Likewise, I did.

A Scandal at the Theater des Westens

I was to appear in a revue that was deplorable. Despite the fact that it was assembled in less than a month, my name was the focal point of all the publicity. The management placed the blame on me when the performance failed.

In the event that the revue was pretentious, ugly, and stupid, how could a single performer save the entire production?

The theater management went insolvent, and I was left as their scapegoat.

Nevertheless, my five solo performances were met with thunderous ovation on each successive night, despite the revue's eventual collapse.

They requested that I remain for an additional seven days, making an offer of one thousand marks per night. I consented.

However, Pepito broke into my dressing room on the first day of this extension.

"Stop!" he hollered. A trap. The manager is covertly launching an operetta in this theater tomorrow, while simultaneously employing you to sell tickets. Please gather your belongings; we are departing.

We retrieved my costumes, packed them into two suitcases, and departed. I neglected to eliminate my makeup.

The theater descended into pandemonium as we departed in a taxi at a rapid pace. The audience, anticipating the performance, became increasingly agitated and enraged. Their murmurs evolved into shouting, which subsequently evolved into riots.

The auditorium was evacuated by two hundred police officers.

Tickets were refunded at random, and even those on the guest list were able to receive twenty marks.

Berlin—A City That Is Unique

Berlin continued to be one of the most aesthetically pleasing capitals in the world, despite the disorder. There was no city that managed daily existence more effectively.

The workers were well-mannered, the officers were polite, and the hospitality was refined to an unsettling degree.

The elegance of Berlin's women astounded me, to the extent that I frequently observed them at my own cabaret on Behrenstrasse.

The Kurfürstendamm was a glistening boulevard in West Berlin that was more intense than Paris at night.

Grand cafés and restaurants are reminiscent of ships at sea.

Orchestras played in every location—they were gentle, rhythmic, mechanical, and hypnotic.

I was captivated by two locations in Berlin.

A world of mute wonder—the aquarium at the zoo.

And Vaterland—a vast hall in which each nation had its own restaurant, theater, and specialty. A metropolis within a city.

Germany's Diverse Aspects: Beyond Berlin

I had the pleasure of performing at the Friedrichsbau Theater in Stuttgart for two weeks, and it was a delightful and pleasant success.

I shared the stage with an exotic animal performance at the Krystallpalast in Leipzig.

Three diminutive crocodiles entered my dressing room one evening, waggishly waving their tails.

I have a deep affection for animals; however, I am not fond of the way they applaud me with their chomping canines.

Germany is an unusual nation. Abundant in contradictions and contrasts.

Nevertheless, the theaters were consistently packed.

Josephine was praised by them each evening.

Munich—A City That Refused Me

"Madame, you will not be dancing in Munich."

The police were resolute, despite my protests. "Munich is a city that is respected."

Consequently, I refrained from dancing in Munich.

Munich, the oldest and most proud of German cities, was envious of its traditions. It was proud of its grand squares, wide avenues, and the Deutsches Museum, a massive archive of human invention that spanned twenty kilometers of galleries.

Upon my arrival, I was enveloped in furs and anticipated that Munich's audiences would provide me with warmth through their acclaim, as the temperature was twenty-two degrees below zero. However, I was confronted with rejection.

"No, Mademoiselle, you are the epitome of immorality."

The authorities had communicated.

Munich was like a dethroned capital, unsure of its identity, populated by Americans and steamed cuisine. Nevertheless, I derived pleasure from its beer halls—at least, they did not prohibit me from consuming alcohol.

Hamburg—A Distinct Greeting

Hamburg, on the other hand, welcomed me.

The Hansa-Theater was a prime example of efficiency, a flawless European music hall in which all operations were executed with precision. By 10:30 PM, I was in bed, a rare luxury, as I had gone onstage early.

"Ich Küsse Ihre Hand, Madame" was a resounding triumph during my performance in Hamburg. Hamburg extended an extraordinary greeting to me while Munich closed its doors.

I also encountered August, a delightful newborn elephant at the menagerie. Hagenbeck's animal sanctuary, a wonder of wild creatures, is of course located in Hamburg.

At that time, I received a peculiar business proposal in the form of a letter from an individual who desired to capture and sell untamed animals from Africa. What is his strategy? To direct all lions, panthers, and other animals to a central location, and subsequently sell them in Germany and America. He desired that I make an investment.

I should have forwarded his letter to Hagenbeck.

In addition to the theaters, Hamburg's port and cabaret district captivated me. A forest of cranes and masts, endless quays, and ships departing for unknown destinations.

At that point, my European voyage concluded. It was time to sail south, across the ocean, toward Argentina and Brazil.

A Controversial Firestorm in Argentina

I sailed past Italy in spring 1929, leaving behind marble cities and snow-capped mountains.

I observed Europe diminishing on the horizon from the deck of the Conte Verde. The longest crossing of my life—fourteen days between the heavens and the sea. Long days of infinite conversations, wireless music, cocktails, and deck chairs.

Afterward, Buenos Aires—the most modern and opulent city in South America. A city that is constructed on squares that are precisely measured, with streets that form a geometric grid.

I arrived to both scandal and magnificent publicity. I was depicted as a femme fatale, a demon, and a scandalous force of devastation, as was the case in Central Europe. Rumors circulated that I consumed blood, consumed live rabbits, and preserved their feet as fortunate charms.

President Yrigoyen, a man renowned for his uncompromising morality, condemned me unequivocally. La Calle denounced me, while Crítica defended me, and my name was prominently featured in the newspapers. The theater doors were the scene of violent altercations, and my performances were transformed into a battlefield as political factions engaged in a pitched battle.

A riot broke out on the 50th night, during which firecrackers were detonated beneath the seats, women collapsed, and males engaged in physical altercations. The curtain rose and fell in a state of hysteria. Protesters chanted:

"Yrigoyen must be defeated!"

"May Yrigoyen continue to thrive!"

Nevertheless, the orchestra continued to perform, drowning out the pandemonium with ferocious tangos.

The theater was still packed every night by the 200th performance. Shaking but ecstatic, the impresario acknowledged:

"I have never earned more money than I have with Miss Baker."

He ought to have expressed gratitude to Yrigoyen.

A Journey Through Argentina I embarked on a journey inland from Buenos Aires:

Liquid gold spills from sacks onto docks in Rosario, a city that is heavy with the fragrance of wheat.

Córdoba, a city that is very profoundly Catholic, extended a warm welcome to me. A newborn cougar was even presented to me by a resident. Regrettably, it perished.

Returning to Buenos Aires, the situation had stabilized. I performed at four distinct venues: Astral, Fenix, Empire, and Florida.

I attended a gathering at La Peña, a meeting place for artists that is managed by a Frenchman, prior to my departure. This was always a source of solace for me while traveling.

The tangos of Buenos Aires mesmerized me. Three songs were sung by me

"Garufa," "Haragán," and "Mama Yo Quiero un Novio."

The weight of love, loss, and longing is carried by tango, which, like the ocean, travels with its own rhythm.

Uruguay—A Country of Compassion

I arrived in Montevideo, which is situated two hundred kilometers from Buenos Aires, after crossing the Río de la Plata.

Uruguay was more friendly, tranquil, and accommodating than Argentina. No uprisings, no scandals—only ecstatic audiences and benevolent journalists.

I observed an unusual phenomenon at the Urquiza Theater: the women were seated in a grand balcony known as the cazuela, which was separate from the males. It evoked memories of the harems of the past in Turkey.

Women would present me with arrangements of violets each evening from this balcony. Now, these dried violets occupy the pages of my books, nestled between Edgar Wallace's offenses.

Montevideo idolized me, and I reciprocated the sentiment. Upon my attempt to depart, they draped me in flowers, transforming me into a strolling bouquet.

Chile—A Land of Contrasts

I was required to traverse the Andes in order to reach Chile, a perilous and breathtaking voyage.

The air became thinner at an altitude of 3,200 meters, causing women to swoon in their carriages. While the train staff hurried with oxygen tanks, I gazed at the cliffs above and the abyss below, ensnared between the earth and the heavens.

A shrill lament that was more acute than any siren was emitted by an eagle as it circled the train.

The station in Santiago was congested with 20,000 individuals who greeted me. It was reminiscent of Prague or Vienna, but with an even greater urgency. The stationmaster rescued me by concealing me in an antiquated Ford, while the throng shattered windows in their pursuit of Josephine.

I was warmly greeted by President Ibáñez, despite the opposition of Catholic leaders, who guaranteed that I would be able to perform.

Valparaíso, a Monte Carlo by the sea, is where I traveled from Santiago to perform the cueca, a Chilean samba.

I developed a fondness for Chile as my preferred South American nation.

Brazil—A Paradise That Is Unparalleled

Rio de Janeiro is incomprehensible.

A city situated in Guanabara Bay, encircled by 364 garden islands that are scented with flowers. The city is transformed into a shimmering fantasy as the lights reflect off the bay at night.

I stood at the summit of Sugarloaf Mountain, observing the entire scene.

I passed every test in São Paulo, where banana plantations bordered the railway and I performed in front of censors and police.

Coffee and pineapples are the staple crops of Brazil. I tasted feijoada completa, a robust stew that includes black beans, dried meat, and sausages, and was served with a peppery cachaça.

The richest and most attractive beach in the world, Rio's Copacabana Beach, was akin to a paradise. The pavements were adorned with vibrant mosaics, and dancers moved in unison beneath the twinkling lights.

I visited a snake sanctuary in São Paulo, where rattlesnakes were confined for their venom. They starved them in order to generate the most potent poison, which was subsequently harvested drop by drop.

Returning Home

I was summoned home by the French vessel Lutetia following my time in Brazil.

I observed the ocean's changing hues as it sailed, indulging in fresh pineapples and daydreaming of Paris.

My initial grand voyage concluded.

I had departed from Paris. I was on my way back to Paris.

I fervently anticipated that my most significant accomplishment would be present.

4

A CINEMATIC TURN

Cinema: A World of Light and Shadow

Negro art, which encompasses images, dance, sun, and darkness, is also present in contemporary cinema. I aspire to have my own home cinema, absent of a telephone or wireless connection—the telephone is such a nuisance! I would prefer to observe rather than listen.

I embarked on my film voyage with Monsieur Nalpas for the Folies revue. I stared directly into the set lights, despite the fact that they blinded me. Eventually, I would produce films that were exclusively composed for me, beginning with a screenplay by Maurice Dekobra.

A Stranger with a Proposal

One day, an enigmatic individual emerged—one of those figures that perpetually lurked behind the scenes, slipping into dressing rooms and quietly observing from the shadows. A mediator, possibly of Russian descent, who was well-versed in Dekobra.

Dekobra, who was both engaging and brimming with ideas, expressed a desire to compose an extraordinary screenplay for me. I was inexperienced, youthful, and self-assured. Life has since instilled in me the importance of prudence; however, I harbor no animosity toward him.

I acquired not only the ability to speak French, but also the ability to comprehend the fixers of the world.

Thrown into the filming process without any prior knowledge of swimming

Tell me, Monsieur Sauvage, are you capable of swimming?

Consider being tossed into a body of water without any knowledge of how to navigate. I was compelled to enter the cinema, with the expectation of surviving.

There was no director to instruct me, no guidance, and no training I received. They anticipated that my name would suffice for all purposes. However, cinema is not defined by the mere act of swaying on stage. I was compelled to adjust. I found it difficult.

I would be found culpable of inexperience if I were to stand trial for my early films, but I would not be held accountable. There is an expense associated with acquiring experience.

Cinema—A Love That Emerges from the Shadows

I grew up listening to tales about graveyards.

What is the reason for the obsessive care that African Americans have for cemeteries? The stones sway in the pale moonlight, and the deceased emerge as silhouettes, striving to accomplish what they were unable to in life.

These shades were both beloved and terrifying during my upbringing. Then, new hues emerged, originating from literature: history, myths, and crime novels—oh, crime novels! Real novels are the sole ones that interest me.

I intentionally read them at night, invoking fear in the same manner as an old acquaintance.

Monsieur Sauvage, do you not believe that visions are comparable to cinema? Black-and-white images that flicker in the dark, revealing truths that we scarcely comprehend.

Shadows from childhood, literature, and dreams haunt me as I awaken in the middle of the night. As I activate the lighting, they disperse. And then, the house is the only thing that remains, gleaming like a screen after the show has concluded.

Cinema was the subsequent progression.

Power of Expression

During my childhood, I combined the bright hues of the screen with the more somber hues of my memories.

Have you observed the manner in which I invoke a memory by indicating to my foot prior to dancing? Our digits and eyes must be in accordance with every aspect of our being.

However, our bodies are lifeless, and our features are frozen. What is the reason for the inability to move our nostrils, ears, and toes? Why do we regard our faces as if they were masks?

I gaze at the thousands of faces in front of me while on stage, contemplating the following:

"It is your responsibility to animate them to make them move."

Cinema: A Sequence of Images

A ballet is a film, but it differs from one performed on a stage. Early cinema failed in this regard by filming music hall revues without altering them.

In the realm of cinema, pace is paramount. the rhythm of a film captivates the pulse and maintains attention. However, the magic of cinema has been somewhat diminished by the introduction of talking pictures, which have resulted in spirits with booming voices.

Nevertheless, I visited the cinema in every country, observing every exceptional film. I aspire to create a genuine film, a beautiful one, one day, as cinema is the embodiment of truth, don't you?

My Initial Films: A Failure

I did not read the screenplay for Siren of the Tropics; it was not even translated for me. Even worse, they composed it during the filming.

Prior to that, I captured an even odd event: a Charleston recording.

According to history—or legend—I introduced the Charleston to Europe. They wrote the most absurd things about it, as if I had annihilated the quadrille, childhood, and the West itself!

However, what about that film? A catastrophe.

I danced without any guidance, direction, or comprehension of angles or cosmetics. Additionally, cinema necessitates angles, cadence, and exaggeration, much like theater and music hall. Success is achieved by adapting, not by reiterating the same strategy.

Missed Opportunity

I experienced my second failure when I filmed the Folies revue in 1926.

However, prior to that, Joe Alex, a colored artist, conceived a vision: a film company that would cater to Black artists in France.

He inquired, "What are your thoughts?"

"I adore it!" I exclaimed.

We devised a plan for weeks; our future was to be in the realm of noir film.

And then...we ceased discussing it.

A pity. Paris boasts exceptional Black artists; however, their utilization remains unknown.

Cinematic blindness

My initial day on set was characterized by dazzling spotlights, burning eyes, and a lack of guidance.

"Reduce." Commence anew. Please refrain from gazing at the camera, madam.

Nothing was visible to me. For days, my eyeballs were on fire.

And then, in Siren, they transported me to the tropics, where I was clad in a fur suit. Nothing about me was comprehended by them.

I am enraged by the squandered opportunities and dismal films that could have been exceptional. What is the rationale for manipulating reality? The Fontainebleau forest purported to be my wild Antilles, but nature is unyielding—you could discern the ruse.

Landscapes are also actors.

Story of the Siren

Consequently, I assumed the identity of Papitou, the Siren of the Tropics.

I portrayed a girl who aspires to introduce a novel dance form to Europe in various locations, including the Natan studio, Théâtre Mogador, Fontainebleau, and a "Negro village" constructed for the film in Épinay.

She discards her empty purses due to her lack of funds. She provides a talisman; however, railway companies do not accept lucky charms, and they should, as calamity is imminent.

Despite her determination, she manages to board a vessel; however, the journey is beset by a series of misfortunes.

She is plunged into a coal hold and emerges in a state of complete darkness. Subsequently, she conceals herself within a flour canister and emerges in a ghostly white state. An elderly Englishwoman experiences a loss of consciousness.

A film that is replete with color, or at least as much color as black and white can accommodate.

Cinema—A Dream That Has Not Yet Been Realized

Although my initial films were unsuccessful, they served as a valuable lesson in the importance of avoiding certain mistakes.

I now yearn for a genuine film that is a reflection of my personality, in which I have the ability to shape my image, and that recounts a true story.

Cinema is not merely an entertainment medium for me. It is a location where shadows can dance, where visions can manifest, and where the truth can be observed.

And one day, I will create a film that is deserving of the name Josephine Baker.

Cinema and Its Absurdities

Monsieur Sauvage, why do film correspondents persist in penning meaningless, unsubstantiated narratives during the production of a film? The alleged news articles regarding Siren of the Tropics were occasionally amusing and occasionally irritating—a common occurrence in the realm of idiocy.

A prime example is as follows:

A breathless woman, who has ascended seventy-eight steps to the studio, blunders into the set and inquires, "Madame, what are you filming today?"

"Today, La Sirène des trois piqués," I purportedly replied in delightful, broken French. (The Siren of the Three Crazies, rather than The Siren of the Tropics.)

"Three individuals who are mentally unstable?" She pointed to two actors who were amusing themselves, exclaiming, "I only see two!" "Where is the third?"

Allegedly, I directed my attention to a fire officer and stated, "He is not insane; he is simply lazy." A firefighter who is slugg

This absurdity was published in a French newspaper. Just imagine!

Movies and Money

I harbor a strong aversion to stinginess, but I am equally repelled by money. I have discovered this the hard way: a director who is fixated on cost-cutting produces subpar films. Although some of my films generated revenue, I received minimal compensation. I would not have been concerned if the films had been of superior quality; however, this was irrelevant.

First Aid and Accidents

I frequently served as the first-aid provider on the set. I assisted Georges Melchior in limping and Pierre Batcheff in tumbling down boulders. For this reason, I hold the Sisters of Charity in high regard.

In reference to Melchior, I recall the profound emotion he experienced while observing me in our final scene. He recognized my potential; however, it was too late. Kranine, Alex, and his dog were the only individuals who genuinely comprehended my situation.

Film Improvisation

Under six gargantuan spotlights at Mogador, I donned a salmon-pink leotard that was both excessively long and loose. The audience was densely crowded with skeptical critics.

I removed the bottom of my leotard in the middle of the scene, contacted my dresser to repair my accessories, and continued dancing.

The audience let out a collective exclamation, and it was evident that some were exceedingly pleased.

Cinema is preposterous.

While at Éclair Studios, they constructed a Negro village for Siren. They captured Madame Récamier, a scene in which aristocrats marched to the guillotine, in the neighboring building. A scene of princes and marchionesses sipping tea in close proximity to jungle huts—what an experience!

Indulging in extravagant descriptions, a journalist described another set as resembling "an Assyrian temple, an ultra-fantastical nightclub, and a suspension bridge for a jazz band—lined with stuffed monkeys."

He described it as "a tropical orgy as Parisian."

Cinema is genuinely a form of madness.

Beauty, Ugliness, and Camera Appeal

I could converse for hours about the camera's perception of attractiveness; however, I have already discussed the topic of facial expressions to an excessive extent. Therefore, we should proceed.

A Night in Budapest

I was requested to perform during the intermission while they were presenting Siren in Budapest.

Mistinguett was visible in a private enclosure as I stood before the screen. What a remarkable character! "What an artist!"

I directed my attention to her and declared, "How could you have failed to recognize that the beloved Parisian is present with us tonight?" Let us unite in shouting: Vive Mistinguett! "Vive Paris!"

The audience erupted in cheers, shouting, "Vive Mistinguett!" "Vive Paris!"

Additionally, as is customary, they chanted, "Ra, ra, ra!" three times, followed by the chant "Vive la Hongrie!"

Mistinguett was evidently moved. In the genuine spirit of a showgirl, she threw the flowers I had brought her into the audience.

Wow, what a mystical evening.

The Lessons of Cinema

I believed that cinema introduced me to the concept of being a Negro.

'One Negro here,' Marc Allégret would call. "There is a black individual over there..."Please retrieve the Negro.

I searched for this "Negro" until I discovered that they were referring to the blackboard used for note-taking.

I was in the process of filming my first talkie, Zouzou, at the time. I had not previously entertained the notion of aural films. What enables mere shadows to speak, chant, and shout with such authenticity? However, I witnessed it occur during a boxing match in Vienna in 1929. The shouts of the audience were captured and replayed in a clear, dynamic manner. That was the moment when I comprehended.

Creating Zouzou

Zouzou was photographed in Paris and Toulon from June to August 1934.

The narrative was straightforward: Jean Gabin portrays my brother, who is not actually my brother. I am infatuated with him without being aware of it. However, he is infatuated with Yvette Lebon, and our father, Pierre Larquey, is facing financial difficulties.

"You are destined for comedy," they informed me. "You are incapable of portraying a woman."

Certainly! I did not object; I preferred to remain true to myself.

I caused a disturbance by playing practical pranks and causing mischief, such as declaring, "You are the devil!"

In one scenario, I am employed in a laundry facility, where I am responsible for ironing the undergarments of a music hall celebrity. She is replaced by me at a later time.

Suddenly, the audience is taken aback as I drop the iron and drape myself in the petticoat of another individual. The audience then erupts in a manner reminiscent of a pie crust that is rising.

Music, dancing, and lights—oh, la la!

Comedy as Tragedy

Cinematic illusions are perpetually disrupted by the realities of life.

Zouzou, a diminutive black dog, was my fortunate charm prior to the commencement of filming. He was consistently present in my life.

Subsequently, he disappeared, along with my luggage, one evening.

I reassured myself, "I am not concerned with the bag; however, I am eager to retrieve my Zouzou."

Neither of them returned.

I found solace in the thought that the criminal may have had an affinity for animals.

Films featuring animals

In one scenario, I pass by a shop window that contains a caged bird. To ensure that they are capable of flight, I am adamant about employing genuine birds.

However, the birds declined to depart.

They were indifferent to freedom as they hopped on their perches. Their seeds were their preference.

I was devastated. I did not receive any response when I jolted the cage.

A stray dog was also present in another scene. I was instructed to activate a hydrant, allow it to drip, and observe the unfortunate creature consume the water. However, the dog was genuinely parched, and I opened the hydrant to full force—a geyser!

All individuals—actors, personnel, and passersby—were waterlogged. However, the cinematographer was delighted with it.

Biquet's Demise

Biquet was the name of the terrier. He was ill, but the severity of his condition was unknown to us.

I made him a promise: "Promise me a little more time, Biquet." I will invite you to reside with me following this. I will indulge you.

However, Biquet was unable to participate on the final day of filming.

In a corner of the studio, he coiled up.

He had vanished.

I cradled him and wept for him—poor Biquet!

The Magnificence of Jean Gabin

Cinema is a form of entertainment; however, the gravity of real life is underscored by its events, particularly mortality.

This is the reason why Jean Gabin is considered one of the most exceptional actors. He is never able to forget the realities of life and mortality.

On the screen, there is an element of him that transcends the natural; it is preternatural.

However, occasionally, he loses sight of himself...

Scene of the Fight

Teddy Michaud portrayed Julot, the "bad boy," in a single scene.

He compels me to participate in a ritual. I am assigned to bite his hand, and subsequently, Jean assaults him.

Jean made a full commitment—bam, bam! I, too, became engrossed.

I bit Teddy's hand until it was bleeding, rather than merely nibbling on it.

Jean continued to strike.

Teddy appeared bewildered and perplexed.

He was required to be transported to the hospital.

Jean Gabin Nearly Arrested

Jean was nearly apprehended at the Toulon port an hour later.

He entered a café while the filming was suspended, still wearing his sailor's uniform.

A patrol led by a quartermaster passed by.

He yelled, "You there!" "You ought to have returned to the team thirty minutes ago!" We are removing the ensemble."

Jean chuckled.

The quartermaster did not.

Fortunately, an officer who was involved in the production of the film intervened: "Hey, this is Jean Gabin, the actor, Jean Gabin!"

The quartermaster hesitated.

"Why, just now," the officer continued, "he severely assaulted his own friend to the extent that the individual was compelled to seek medical attention."

This was amusing to the genuine mariners.

Additionally, they presented each of us with a beret, which is a token of respect for workers.

A fortunate charm to replace Zouzou.

Zouzou's Publicity and Success

The producers printed Le Journal de Zouzou, a newspaper with a 600-copy circulation, during the filming process.

I discovered that my "greatest aspiration" was to possess a bed in the same size as Marie Antoinette's.

I had never considered it previously. I was unable to suppress my curiosity: What was the appearance of Marie Antoinette's bed?

Leaving the Bananas Behind Zouzou was a pivotal moment.

It was the turning point for Viviane Romance and Yvette Lebon.

It served as confirmation of Jean Gabin's exceptional abilities.

And I?

I was not the banana dancer for the first time.

My father was a performer. And I was his daughter.

And at their core, all actors are showmen's offspring.

Even L'Humanité acknowledged that "Zouzou is the sole French music hall film that can compete with American productions."

What more could I possibly desire?

5

AN ENORMOUS APPETITE AND SOFT SKIN

An Offering of Recipes

A Passion for Food and Cooking

I possess an enormous appetite. What is my preferred dish? A dish of Italian spaghetti that has been seasoned with red pepper. I swirl the pepper pot over it for a half hour. It is delectable. I am aware of this because I possess the ability to prepare food.

I frequently prepare meals for my friends, and my repertoire includes American stuffed buns, poultry with cream, fruit tarts, crepes with caviar, jellied rabbit, and Neapolitan macaroni. My crepes with caviar? The most exceptional!

My mother used to say, "You will realize the value of knowing how to cook one day." She was correct.

However, there is one exception: I do not smoke or consume alcohol, with the exception of lager. After attempting to consume alcohol on numerous occasions, I must confess that it did not appeal to me.

A Tribute to Freddy and Four Recipes to Try

I once had a two-meter-tall American chef named Freddy, who was a towering figure with red eyes, a white hat, and a laugh as vast as his appetite. We formed an amusing duo in the basement kitchen, attired in our white aprons and working in tandem.

In memory of Freddy, who has an even greater passion for cuisine than I do, I have compiled a list of four recipes that you should consider:

Beauharnais (or Creole) Sweet Potatoes

Peel and boil sweet potatoes with a maximum of two granules of salt.

Drain and puree the potatoes with a small amount of butter, salt, and pepper (one small knob per three potatoes).

Add half a grated coconut and a small amount of milk to the mixture and stir over low heat to achieve a creamy consistency.

Don't be intimidated by the prospect of beating with a fork.

How thin is it? It is a broth. Is it thick? A dessert that can be consumed at any time!

Hotcakes with syrup

Combine one pound of flour, one tablespoon of baking powder, half a liter of milk, two whole eggs, and one tablespoon of melted butter.

Whisk the mixture thoroughly after adding a small amount of salt.

Brown both sides by pouring small quantities onto a hot, greased plate.

Accompany with syrup, marmalade, or butter—you will desire additional servings.

Poached Eggs with Corned Beef Hash

Combine three boiled potatoes, one finely diced onion, and a can of corned beef hash.

Form into mini rolls and cook in a frying pan.

Serve with a thick tomato sauce (I prefer it especially thick!) or a poached egg on top.

Flan by Josephine Baker

Using three scoops of caster sugar, beat three fresh eggs.

Gradually incorporate two tablespoons of flour (or rice flour) into half a liter of milk.

Add three sliced bananas and small pieces of lemon zest, then flavor with two spoonfuls of kirsch.

Bake at a moderate temperature in a flan dish for 20 minutes.

Allow the flan to settle for three hours; you will adore it!

Eat Healthily to Maintain Your Well-Being

Eating nutritiously is essential for maintaining one's health. The more straightforward, the better. Before serving, chew the red flesh thoroughly. It should be rare, juicy, and grilled.

Individuals consume food without digesting, consume medications for all ailments, and continue to experience symptoms of illness. However, health is the most advantageous form of beauty—if only more individuals were aware of this fact!

Beauty, Simplicity, and Superstitions

I am not interested in allowing my identity to be used to promote perfumes, soaps, or cosmetics. What are those chemical compounds in the small jars? Not for me. They induce skin flakiness.

Conversely,

Exercise, dance, and get a good night's sleep. Sleep is more effective than any lotion in clearing the eyes.

Take lengthy steam baths, bathe in violet milk, and use a horsehair brush to scrub your arms daily.

Swim on a daily basis. The elegance of fish will never be matched by land creatures.

The most effective eau de toilette is rainwater; it should be stored in bottles, much like a cosmetic elixir.

For fatigued skin, boil flaxseed water for 15 minutes and apply it to your face both morning and night.

Homemade Beauty Treatments

The skin is softened by the combination of boiled water, cologne, and orange juice in equal portions.

Banana water is effective in reducing creases. This product is made by soaking bananas in alcohol for six days and then diluting the solution.

A rosy complexion is achieved by mashing strawberries or grapes, while fig skin alleviates irritation.

However, attractiveness is not the sole determinant. Do you suffer from rheumatism? The serpent must be skinned alive, but there is an ancient remedy: rattlesnake fat.

Mama had a straightforward solution for heavy blood, which is detrimental to women: beet leaves cooked in lard with cornbread. Works marvels; you will appear younger!

Superstitions and Hair Magic

Individuals sought to alter my skin coloration to either a darker or lighter shade. I am indifferent to the outcome. Who are the genuine wizards? Hairdressers!

I once composed a love letter to Antoine, the Great Wizard of Hair. My hair was "dressed with caviar" upon my arrival at Rue Cambon, a term used by correspondents to describe the process of slicking it down. Antoine's movements were reminiscent of an elderly St. Louis magician, as he scarcely touched my head.

"Don't think, Mademoiselle, don't do anything that's not harmonious."

I recalled my pirouettes, giraffe walk, and kangaroo walk—movements that were not well-received by others, but which possessed a unique harmony.

Eventually, I mustered the courage to search. Antoine had converted my hair into a garden, incorporating glazed spirals, leaves, and flowers. I was too embarrassed to embrace him, so I decided to send him that letter.

Currently, Antoine is the proprietor of a hairstyling empire in New York. Jean Clément once presented me with a triple bun, which consisted of three buns that were piled in a manner reminiscent of a sculpture. Each hairstyle is a unique disguise that influences the individual's identity. More significant than an outfit!

Superstitions? I have faith in them.

Do not whistle in my dressing room; it is a symptom of death.

Avoiding the consumption of animal skulls may result in headaches.

Knives and utensils should never be crossed.

Presenting a weapon as a gift? You have recently severed a friendship.

It is considered unlucky to transport burning timber, while cinders are considered sacred.

Sewing is prohibited on Thursdays and Saturdays.

And most importantly, refrain from pursuing financial gain. It is a liquid that easily passes through your palms. The smile of an acquaintance is far more valuable than the 100,000 francs I possess.

Women, Freedom, and the Future

What does the future contain for women? I am unaware of the future, nor am I aware of the present.

However, one thing is evident:

A businessman is a man. They are fixated on women.

Women are never able to ignore their gender. and they are increasingly employing it.

I have a personal aversion to lax women, particularly those who attempt to be sincere. I either adore someone or I do not.

In terms of the future?

I am optimistic that we will share a life without clothing.

However, how many of us—whether we are male or female—are genuinely capable of doing so?

6

HOW I BECAME A SINGER

From Rue Pigalle to the Club des Champs-Élysées, and Cabarets

The Inception of My Cabaret

I used to dance at the Abbaye de Thélème, the Impérial, or the Milonga every night after my performances. However, it was difficult to dance on all fours, squeeze between tables, or use only my limbs. Montmartre was a chaotic place at midnight; individuals consumed you with their gaze.

Therefore, I considered the possibility of establishing my own cabaret. That is precisely what I did on December 14, 1926.

I had never experienced such an abundance of enjoyment. I interacted with all members of the establishment, including the stewards, the maître d', the chef, and even the goat and the pig, by joking, stroking bald heads, pulling beards, and dancing. Charleston, samba, and swing—it was insane. All night, I threw streamers, popped balloons, and played with lights until I found myself in tears of laughter. I would consume supper at five in the morning.

On occasion, I would dance for an uninterrupted eighteen hours on Sundays.

Obstacles and Contrary Facts

White males are peculiar.

I would perform every evening at the Abbaye de Thélème and would always return home alone. This suggests that there is still a lack of comprehension among Caucasian individuals.

I contracted pneumonia for the first time during my tenure there. A monstrous creature, jostling me as violently as a coconut tree. People lost faith, believing that I had already vanished. I also encountered it independently.

Observe me as I dance; I am not a part of the audience and do not belong onstage. In a circle of applauding hands, dance should be performed in the center of the audience, where all participants are on the same level and in the same light.

However, when I am not dancing or when I am ailing, please refrain from approaching me.

The World of Cabaret and Chez Joséphine

Chez Joséphine, my inaugural cabaret, was inaugurated on Rue Pigalle. I was not compensated; however, I was provided with sustenance. Additionally, I encountered soufflés—oh, what a blast! Cheese soufflé, mushroom, vanilla, chocolate, rum... I nearly experienced indigestion; however, I have no remorse.

I departed one month later.

I felt at home among cloth dolls—Josephines with crossed eyes, just like mine—at a cabaret that Pepito managed on Rue Fontaine. I held them in my arms as we danced.

I entertained patrons at the Acacias tearoom, which is situated in close proximity to Place de l'Étoile, in the afternoons. The location became quite scandalous, as it was populated by American women who were transiting through and gigolos who used silk handkerchiefs to wipe lipstick stains.

I had never considered the potential revenue that could be generated from heated water. We would plunge the same teabag into five pots, ensuring that the water was tinted just enough. Naturally, it is now customary for each individual to possess their own teabag. However, at that time? Dip, then serve! Everyone was content.

Developing as a vocalist

I would not have attempted to sing in public at that time. I would croon while playing with the cat at home—just la la la, ti ti ti, nothing more.

However, my companions exerted pressure on me on Rue Fontaine:

"Josephine, sing!"

"Give us a song!"

"Josephine…!"

I anticipated that they would cause damage to the club, including glasses, ashtrays, and ice containers.

All right. I sang. It was a horrible experience. I gagged.

However, I gradually adapted to it. I initiated the process of improvisation. And that is how I became a singer.

What was the first song I ever performed in public? Adorable infant.

In the interim, my pig, which had been spoiled by the cabaret's leftovers, had become so corpulent that he could no longer fit beneath the furnace where he was sleeping. One night, in a fit of exasperation, he lifted the entire structure, including the pipes. He eventually grew to such a size that he was unable to pass through the kitchen entrance. In order to extract him, we were required to demolish a portion of the wall.

The unfortunate swine! He was akin to a rolling barrel, his antennae sweeping the floor.

From a Silent Star to a Music Hall Star

I was still merely a silent performer at the Folies Bergère, a nude attraction outside the cabaret.

Monsieur Henri Varna, the artistic director of the Casino de Paris, was the individual responsible for altering this. He observed something in me that transcended mere swaying. I received my position as a music hall icon from him.

I always formed friendships with my theater supervisors. However, the situation was not the same with Monsieur Varna. His mother, a delightful woman, had faith in me prior to any other individual. She maintained her conviction that "This girl will be a star" when critics dismissed me, stating, "Her body is spectacular, but that's not enough."

Monsieur Varna, being a virtuous son, deferred to his mother's advice.

He employed me. This craft was imparted to me by him. But more importantly, he was able to safeguard the qualities that defined me. He never coerced me into becoming someone I was not. He had confidence in me.

I was trembling and feeling disoriented during my initial appearance on the Casino stage. Subsequently, the thunderous applause ensued. I raced forward, shouting, "Thank you!" as I was overwhelmed. I am grateful. I am extremely grateful, ladies and gentlemen.

Monsieur Varna replied, "No, my dear." "You are not a street performer." Do not express your gratitude in such a manner. You are no longer a member of a cabaret. Observe me... Bow to the right and to the left with grace and magnificence. Now, you are the center of attention.

Nevertheless, I have consistently embraced my audience. They are my family. They are aware of when you are being truthful. Additionally, they are fond of receiving affection.

Monsieur Derval and the Folies

Monsieur Derval was present at the Folies, and the situation was distinct. He was an expert in artistic direction, surpassing all others in the United States. I am not making any exaggerations. No matter how extravagant or grandiose, his productions were mathematical.

Theater was a laboratory under his leadership. Precision prevailed in the backstage area. No one was left to chance.

Directors are seldom comprehended by audiences. They envision them as something else. Despite his tall, robust, and almost brusque appearance, Monsieur Derval was a sensitive individual, reminiscent of a child. A director is incapable of engaging an audience without possessing profound sensitivity.

His wife was equally remarkable—a perfectionist with fabrics, hues, and frills, she was elegant and tireless. One who is a tyrant with furnishings. I have an aversion to measurements.

"Raise your arm." Kneel. Rotate your cranium. One pin, two pins, three, ten, thirty pins...

I am not a pincushion.

My Evolving Environment

Before transferring Rue Fontaine to Jane Aubert, whom I held in high regard, I resided there for two years. Her status as a celebrity preceded my own. At the Abbaye de Thélème, I could hear her. She evoked a sense of hopelessness in me; she was so natural and engaging on stage.

In 1937, during the Colonial Exposition, Chez Joséphine Baker relocated to Rue François 1er. A more tranquil location, which is jammed with individuals from all over the world each evening.

They had not yet considered the possibility of conflict.

I sang "Pretty Little Baby." or something more eerie:

"Suppose…"

Then, war appeared.

The pleasure was altered. It was no longer unadulterated. Nightclubs underwent a transformation, becoming increasingly tense and resembling viper pits. However, it is also more impressive. More expressive.

The vernacular itself underwent a transformation. The term "cabaret" was no longer used. The term contracted amid the tide of history.

They exclaimed, "Let's go to the club!"

And so they arrived—to hear me at Club 48, Club 49, and the Club des Champs-Élysées.

I was pinned against a pillar, singing as if to myself, as I stood beneath frigid lights:

"C'est à minuit que tout paraît surnaturel…"

"It's at midnight that everything seems supernatural."

Paris. Paris. Paris.

Monsieur Spaak, the Belgian prime minister, extended an invitation to me to join him at his table at the club. He was benevolent.

The King and Queen of Belgium were also present, although they were disguised; however, they were recognized by all. The maître d' hesitated. The florist experienced a state of paralysis. However, they were waived past by the King and Queen. They were exceedingly benevolent.

Rita Hayworth and Aly Khan, sitting in close proximity to the orchestra, were quite endearing.

Emperor Bao Dai, who maintained his hair in a similar manner to mine, paused to listen. He cradled his matchbox with the same care as a precious object. As he listened, even the spent match in his fingertips appeared precious.

"Mais oui, mais oui, pardi, ce que j'en dis on vous l'a déjà dit…"

"But yes, but yes, of course, I've told you what you already know…"

"But that's Paris."

7

FROM THE STAGE TO THE GRAMOPHONE

From Negro Songs to "Ave Maria"

Gramophones are my passion. I have experimented with every brand in existence. At the outset, my voice was featured on seven Odeon recordings. Do you share their sentiments?

"Who?" "Dinah," "That Certain Feeling"...

I was unable to forget the sensation I experienced the first time I encountered you, and I nearly fell to the ground."Sleepy Time Gal," "I Wonder Where My Baby Is Tonight"...

I believed that burning all of my old correspondence would alleviate my distress. However, I continue to be uncertain as to her whereabouts this evening.

..."Bam Bam Bamy Shore," "I Want to Yodel," and "You Are the Only One"... Furthermore, I am particularly fond of these two songs:

Not for a single hour Not for a single day Not for a single year

However, this is the case perpetually.

In order to comprehend authentic Negro songs, it is necessary to navigate the Mississippi River on one of those antique paddlewheel vessels. Forests, farmlands, and marshes, which are bubbling with hot gases, pass by the riverbanks as the gigantic paddlewheels slowly turn at night. Negroes sit like statues along the river, singing their ancient melodies. Their voices are sometimes tender and soft, like whispers in the dark, and sometimes short and passionate, full of shouts and vigorous movements.

They frequently sing ancient African melodies without realizing it, such as the one my friend once recorded for me:

AHAN'S SONG

Hi-Ho-Mang' Moussa,

chant, chant, paddler in front,

The sailors on the water were deeply troubled.

Oh, my! The immense sorrow, Of the black men, Of the black men on the water...

Monsieur Sauvage, does it not evoke the melodies of the Russian boatmen? It is unfortunate that we do not possess the melody. Europeans would impose strict rhythms on these songs, but they fail to comprehend that these melodies can only follow their own rhythm—the rhythm of the night, the location, and the blood coursing through the singer.

These melodies are akin to medicine: they alleviate pain, alleviate exhaustion, and alleviate sorrow. They are virtually impossible to translate literally, much like American songs that are derived from Negro tunes that resist precise translation. However, I will attempt it.

MANAMA'S MOURNING

The moon is a thief, Stealing away my beloved, Love arrived, Death arrived with love...

UKULELE LADY

I observed the beauty of the moonlight on Honolulu Bay. Girls cradled their ukuleles along the shores, and they sang a tender melody beneath the soft radiance of the moon.

A song is not merely a collection of melodies that are unraveled with a forced smile, nor is it a mere lament or a reckless performance. It is a drama, a sequence of movements, and a demonstration of emotions. Music has the ability to shape you the way a sculptor shapes an object in the air; your voice must harmonise with your body. You sing with your knees, elbows, shoulders, and every other part of your body.

Each tune necessitates its own hairstyle, costume, lighting, and scenery. An artist must extract every ounce of emotion from a composition, akin to juicing a lemon. However, this does not necessitate a frenzied leap. Even the largest audience can be moved by a subtle, genuine bow.

Once, I had a desire to sing on my knees alone at the center stage of the Casino de Paris, and I succeeded. However, Monsieur Sauvage, that posture had to be authentic. Nothing functions when all elements are synthetic. The audience is moved by the shared silence in which every pulse appears to beat in unison; they yearn to hear your heartbeat in the silence between notes. The most challenging accomplishment in performance art is the instant when the entire room simultaneously holds its breath.

It is exclusively available to those who exert themselves without forfeiting their inherent spontaneity.

My inspiration has always been derived from an extraordinary woman: Mistinguett. Although she may have been ridiculed by others, it is impossible to dispute that she has never aged. She has dedicated herself to the continuous improvement of her art through the application of real-world experiences.

Whenever I am on the brink of giving up and feel fatigued, I reflect on her and summon the fortitude to persevere. I advise myself to labor diligently, as she does, and to experience life to the fullest. Maybe no one in our generation can supplant Mistinguett. The cheers that erupt upon her arrival at a performance as an audience member are a testament to the enduring place she holds in the hearts of people.

In light of the numerous rumors that have been circulated about her, I would like to convey one fact: she was exceedingly benevolent toward her family. Everything else is solely idle gossip and misunderstanding.

I apologize, Monsieur Sauvage, for attaching such significance to the charity of an artist. The voice that emanates from within is of paramount importance to me. The lament of the Little Sparrow was possessed by Édith Piaf. I may not be the most accurate assessor of her artistry, as I am not sufficiently fluent in French to truly appreciate the influence of her accent. However, she is without a doubt the most feminine of our chanteuses.

She was modest, empathetic, and forthright when we initially encountered her at her American cabaret. I was immediately impressed by her. I perceived her as a kind individual.

What is the reason for the scarcity of compassion in the present day? The world is not merely unbecoming; it is intolerable. Everything must be rectified and transformed with compassion. Who is responsible for the welfare of low-level employees? This is an issue that cannot be resolved by machines.

There is an immense amount of suffering experienced by young artists. It is effortless to assert that a seventeen-year-old female has an insatiable appetite for theater; however, passion does not guarantee sustenance. They are compelled to become someone's concubine in order to survive, are underpaid, and are often placed in desperate situations. The arts, as well as their own future, are being condemned by directors, who are culpable of this. I am sickened, and my pleasure is drained.

A song is a lullaby that we adhere to in life, whether it is sad, funny, or dramatic. Hope is a window that is accessible. However, even the most forthcoming individuals are never sufficiently forthcoming.

Given that all things must eventually come to an end, let us at least endeavor to avoid squandering our time...

A song is a performance that brings a character to life. However, you must first acquire luck—a melody and the appropriate chorus. I was fortunate to have Vincent Scotto, who provided me with compositions that were in accordance with my intended message. The lyrics? Frequently lacking in strength. What is the reason for the lack of songwriting by poets? What is the reason for the departure of vocalists from their stage personas? It emanates an absence of vitality.

Theater is a reflection of life—exaggerated yet consistently accurate. I was taught that more effectively by Sacha Guitry than by any other individual. He is the most exceptional theater actor I have encountered, possessing an effortless presence both on and off the stage. Numerous actors maintain an artificial existence, even when they are acting in real life. Guitry, however, remains a human with a sense of style. He comprehended my perspective. He was aware that I was an actress, not merely a "colored frog." It was because of him that I was able to perform in Offenbach's La Créole for a period of ten months.

On December 15, 1934, I performed Jo-la-Terreur on the inaugural night. Every evening, I was compelled to express my anger by smashing vases and dishes—just image the expense today! Fortunately, they were composed of gypsum. Those were enjoyable times. I was reminded of the dresses I would borrow from my grandmother's wardrobe as a child in St. Louis by the oversized sleeves of my costume. I was able to express myself in a variety of ways on stage, including singing, dancing, pulling expressions, roaring, and laughing.

Please recall Jamaica...

The event concluded with a serenade, as I departed the stage with my heart and breath. I was overjoyed to return to Paris after a year and a half of touring, where I was welcomed by a genuine theater audience that was more than just intrigued by my plumage and song. I was assigned a position. The narrative was initiated by me.

La Créole was reworked for my use. It evolved into a voyage, from Jamaica to La Rochelle, much like my own life had been a journey from St. Louis to Paris. I was filled with pride. Appropriately so? Potentially.

However, the most delightful aspect is the children. The play was revitalized by their presence. I provided them with refreshments on Sundays. They informed their mothers, and shortly thereafter, entire families arrived. My dressing room was overrun with infants. I was reminiscent of a nursemaid, as I was enveloped by miniature pink bundles and vials that were scattered throughout the room. It was delightful.

Indeed, melodies possess a soul. It is imperative that you provide them with vitality. However, there are instances in which that essence suffocates you.

When the concentration centers were liberated at the conclusion of the war, they required an individual to sing in a typhoid-infected camp in order to provide hope to the dying. I participated in a volunteer program.

Many of the prisoners collapsed and perished as they clung to the barbed wire, resembling mere skeletons. Those who survived were unable to move and waited. I had never witnessed anything so dreadful. I was aware that the majority would not survive. Nevertheless, they maintained their composure. They made an attempt. Their slender arms were adorned with armbands featuring the Cross of Lorraine. I refrained from weeping. I was compelled to beam. I was obligated to perform.

I sang Dans Mon Village to them in a soft voice, as if I were murmuring to each soul.

In the village where I reside...

Every field, every bush, Every clock tower in the vicinity...

They were expiring, and I observed the clock towers reflected in their eyes. The sound of their labored respiration was reminiscent of distant bells. That facilitated the reestablishment of my voice. Into the melody, I invested my emotional energy. We all wept by the conclusion, not out of sorrow, but because for a brief period, we were no longer sad.

I had sung this hymn in camps throughout Africa and Italy in both French and English until the words lost their significance. The song's essence was what remained. Are you able to comprehend?

I am capable of singing in six languages: French, English, Portuguese, Spanish, Italian, and German. A melody is considered universally accessible once it has been performed in multiple languages. Anything that is excessively specific or mundane is eliminated.

However, Ave Maria was distinct.

People are taken aback by the fact that I, Josephine Baker, perform Ave Maria. I am delighted with it. I am aware of the meaning of the Latin terms, but I am unable to fully comprehend them. Perhaps this is the reason why individuals are moved—the music's essence is the one that is conveyed.

I discovered the core of my Ave Maria in Cairo, where I encountered Father Ayrout, a Jesuit who was dedicated to assisting Egypt's impoverished. He extended an invitation to me to sing in his diminutive chapel, which featured a basic altar and two candles. As I sang, I reflected on the villagers, his devotion to them, and the essence of faith.

That is where I discovered the grace and sincerity of Ave Maria. I now return to that humble altar in Cairo whenever I sing it.

I have previously mentioned that my journey from the Mississippi to the Seine is perpetually on my mind. Isn't it a wonderful adventure, despite all the challenges? A joyful one, in numerous respects?

I continue to perform Ave Maria in Mon Beau Livre d'Images at the Club des Champs-Élysées, albeit in a distinct manner. The exhibition includes humorous, exaggerated illustrations by Albert Dubout. When I observe them, I am unable to suppress my laughter.

However, there is no substitute for live theater. I have worked on recordings and performed on radio, but I despise listening to my own recorded voice. It induces anxiety in me. I produce a sound reminiscent of a ruminant in labor.

Monsieur Gilson, a radio poet, once informed me, "You will be featured on French radio on a weekly basis." I was apprehensive about disappointing him or Monsieur Porché. French radio is the most exceptional; it is more lively and unrestricted than foreign stations, which are exclusively filled with advertisements and business. However, I am unable to function without a live audience.

Television is distinct. There, I am free to express myself through movement and dance. I participated in a televised UN gala in Paris and Café Continental in England.

However, the stage's enchantment is unparalleled—the warmth of an audience, the boards beneath my feet, the radiance of the footlights, the presence of friends. Above all, that is the place where I belong.

8

FOUR YEARS OF ADVENTURE

In the Service of France on the Sidelines of the Second World War

I lived in a state of perpetual motion for four years, alternating between the Château des Milandes, which I had rented prior to the war, and Si Mohamed Menebhi's palace in Marrakesh, in search of refuge between escapades.

The Second World War was a period of adversity, characterized by a fortitude that was unshakable. I was incapacitated, despite the fact that there was no room for illness. "Relax, just one more week... one more month."

It was preposterous. Why not simply provide me with a fastener after thirty-six surgeries? There is no necessity for an infinite number of operations; simply open, verify, and close. Those years were characterized by fevers, clinics, scalpels, and restless nights. The muezzin's every call to prayer was audible to me. I am of the opinion that Muslims are the most closely connected to God. They prayed for me, and

I was able to survive.

The Château des Milandes, which is currently under my ownership, is a castle in Dordogne that was constructed in the fifteenth century. It comprises portions that date back to the twelfth century. It has undergone numerous restorations, yet its medieval allure persists. It provides a panoramic view of the valley where the Dordogne River meanders serenely from its watchtowers. While recuperating in Africa, I studied its history, including the Middle Ages, the Crusades, and the barons of Castelnaud, Milandes, Montfort, and Beynac.

The château was visited by an enigmatic visitor named Jack Sanders on a night in October 1940.

"Who is 'Jack Sanders'?" I inquired.

"Certainly." 'Captain Fox' has passed away. In the near future, "Jack Sanders" will also be included. He will be reborn as Jacques-François Hébert after ten years of age. Please remember.

Jack was a clandestine crusader, serving as Captain Jacques Abtey of the Second Bureau of the General Staff. He was summoned by destiny. He was the most exceptional of the numerous individuals who served France.

What would I have done in their absence? Perhaps I was of assistance to them; however, they were of even greater assistance to me. We made the best of our abilities. However, the pounding pulse! Imagine that I, Monsieur Sauvage, am concealing confidential communications beneath my attire in the manner of miniature hair curlers.

And that was only the beginning.

At the time of our initial encounter, Captain Abtey was known as "Captain Fox." I was acquainted with his family, including his wife and children. They were beloved by me. He initially confronted me in Beau Chêne, my residence in Le Vésinet, which was subsequently occupied and looted by the Germans.

I had always desired to serve France, the nation that had provided me with so much, despite its prejudice. However, I was not an agent. It was not in my character. I was employed by the Red Cross, where I provided assistance to Belgian refugees. Among them were black sheep, individuals who were suspicious and mingled in with the desperate. I observed them. I attentively heard.

An Italian embassy attaché had a proclivity for murmuring in my ear. He disclosed information to me, which I communicated to Captain Fox. It delighted him.

Despite the autumn cold, we felt secure at the Château des Milandes. Then, in September 1940, there was a loud explosion, a bang, and a bang. a loud banging at the door. An officer and three riflemen flanked a German soldier who stood in the vicinity.

"You are concealing weapons within this château..." We are aware.

Oh, that's right! He was exceedingly formal and reserved. Every exit was barred by his men. However, the château was devoid of armaments.

I am relieved. An armchair is precisely what you require following such an excursion.

Jack informed me that French intelligence was in the process of restructuring. British intelligence was intervening. Additionally, Josephine Baker, a prominent figure on the stage, could prove advantageous for covert operations.

All right, children. We should organize an event. You will be proficient in the flute. Jack is, after all, an artist. A maestro of ballet.

We embarked on a journey to Brazil, Portugal, and Spain. However, passports were not distributed in the same manner as Metro tickets. The trains made their way toward the boundary at a glacial pace, never reaching the desired speed.

Toulouse, Lourdes, Tarbes, Pau, the Pyrenees, and customs.

"Please provide your passports."

Everything appeared to be proceeding smoothly.

A Douglas aircraft was waiting for us at Barajas airport in Madrid, surrounded by uniforms with swastika markings. The mechanics in blue overalls were benevolent toward me. Rotors rotated. It is now time to depart.

A Spanish plane, which was diminutive in size, maneuvered in close proximity to us as we took off, executing acrobatics. Would it collide with us? What was its objective? Nothing. Eventually, it vanished.

The moon was suspended in the clouds below.

We were in Portugal when the cabin door opened. Sintra. Sunlight. Individuals who are smiling. There is no conflict.

Hotel Aviz in Lisbon was where I was able to catch my breath. However, the hotel was crowded with journalists.

I assured them that I had nothing to say. "I am merely present to perform music and dance." I am traveling to Rio to sign a contract, and that is all.

I was, however, featured on the front page of every newspaper the following day. I had inadvertently cast a shadow over the Negus's son and King Carol of Romania.

Rio was subsequently canceled. In Lisbon, we were greeted by a dispatch from London, informing us that a new liaison unit was required in France.

Lisbon, I bid you farewell. Jack was confident that I would return, and accordingly, arrangements were made. My documents were secured with the assistance of the Spanish ambassador, who is the brother of the caudillo.

The sky was ominously somber in December. However, there was no time to waste.

I encountered Monsieur Paillole, a critical intelligence connection, upon my return to Marseille. I communicated the information.

I refused to utilize any resources other than my own, as I was financially strapped. Payment is not anticipated in exchange for serving France. Additionally, I had vowed to refrain from singing in France as long as a solitary German remained. However, how would I endure? I was unable to provide a response.

Paillole possessed one.

"Return to the stage." He stated, "It is the most exceptional cover."

Consequently, La Créole, the Offenbach operetta that I had performed in Paris prior to the war, served as my disguise.

I rehearsed the role that I had not played in six years in a mere ten days. Posters were affixed:

On December 24, 1940, Josephine Baker appeared in Offenbach's La Créole.

As I sang "Remember Jamaica," Jack returned with news of an ambitious plan: a small boat that would travel between Lisbon and Casablanca.

La Créole concluded. There will be no more music in Marseille.

I still owed performances in Béziers and Montpellier. Nevertheless, obligation beckoned. I was no longer a volunteer. I was formally conscripted, but I did not receive any compensation or rank. Second-class. Onward! It is necessary to acquire one's stripes.

As I packed my luggage at the Hôtel de Noailles in Marseille, I was coughing very badly. The worst-case scenario was verified by a physician:

"This is a severe matter." You are experiencing pulmonary congestion in its initial stages. Immediately depart from this frigid nation. You require sunlight.

France was encased in snow. 1941 had commenced with a severe beginning.

However, I was unable to depart without my animals. I had made a commitment to them.

Is it possible for someone to retrieve them?

They were retrieved from the château by Bayonne, my team manager. Oh, that's right! What a source of pleasure!

Glouglou, my mischievous monkey, was seeking for fleas in my fur coats. Mica, the golden lion tamarin, was as solemn as a judge. Gugusse, the marmoset, was a genuine rascal, with his tiny mustache. Additionally, there are two diminutive rodents, Mademoiselle Point d'Interrogation and Madamoiselle Bigoudi, who are quite playful.

Then, my Great Dane, Bonzo, who is gentle unless he is misunderstood.

We were a joyful, tumultuous group at the Hôtel de Noailles. Bonzo was sprawled on the rug, with a mouse perched on his snout. An examination of the wardrobe by Gugusse. Glouglou is suspended from the draperies. Mica coiled up on my bed in the manner of a miniature lion.

What a pity! This was also an expedition for them.

It is now time to put them away.

We faced a lengthy journey ahead.

I will always cherish the memory of the voyage from Marseille to Algiers on the Gouverneur Général de Gueydon. What a dreadful weather, Monsieur Sauvage! The animals in my care had never encountered a tempest before, and they certainly acquired knowledge that day. Gugusse anxiously nibbled his small mustache, and Glouglou's irises became dull.

However, the sky was clear upon our arrival, and Algiers was illuminated by the morning sun in a shade of pink.

"Are you Madame Josephine Baker?"

"Certainly, Monsieur."

"Please follow me." A complaint has been filed against you.

The inspector was conducting his duties adequately; however, I was perplexed. May I be apprehended? For what reason?

The Opéra de Marseille had denounced me for breach of contract and requested 400,000 francs in compensation. How benevolent of them! However, their treachery backfired, as I was compelled to remain in Algiers for an additional week and deliver a performance at a banquet for the air force.

I was anticipating my departure to Casablanca. In the interim, I composed letters to consuls on behalf of my dispersed colleagues at the Aletti Hotel, thereby facilitating their missions. At that time, I could not have envisaged that I would soon be traveling across Africa, from Marrakesh to Agadir, from Fez to Spain, Portugal, and back to Morocco. My journey would also take me to Tlemcen, Algiers, Tunis, Tripoli, Benghazi, Alexandria, Cairo, Jerusalem, Damascus, and Beirut. I was unaware of the thousands of kilometers that would be traversed across deserts, roads that were dotted with explosives, and battlefields that were littered with debris. I was also unaware that I would be in a state of limbo for months, this time due to illness rather than conflict.

Nevertheless, there were indicators. Gugusse never returned from his expedition in the hotel's drainage. My diminutive white rodents vanished. I was devastated.

Life is unpredictable; who can anticipate its potential?

I was on a train to Tangier shortly after my arrival in Casablanca, with a suitcase containing theater programs and mundane documents. However, imperceptible messages were concealed between the lines, which were inscribed with a unique ink. My initial objective was to transport it to Lisbon. I was impeccably courteous, composed, and radiating.

In Lisbon, I was safeguarded by prominent Moroccan figures, including Abdulrahman Menebhi, Moulay Larbi el Alaoui's acquaintances, and the highly esteemed Bel Bachir, whose simple presence on the street elicited applause.

A sumptuous banquet was hosted by the Spanish authorities in Tétouan in my honor. If only they had been informed! I listened attentively, capturing every murmured conversation. Josephine was unaware of their presence. They lavished me with gifts, the most valuable of which was a permanent transit visa for Spain...

However, I was not fortunate in Lisbon. Jack's mediator was unsuccessful in achieving the desired outcome, despite a few successful performances—which were included in my cover.

Marrakesh, Monsieur Sauvage—the Pearl of the South, where European and black Africa converge. The ancient walls, towering palm trees, and fountains that are overflowing with crystal-clear water. A city that appears to be the product of the ethereal dreams of desert inhabitants that have endured for centuries.

There, I encountered both pleasure and adversity. I consistently returned to Marrakesh, regardless of my location in Africa. It served as my refuge for four years when I was too fatigued to continue.

The wind, which circulated around the Koutoubia mosque, surged down from the Atlas Mountains.

Donkey drivers in the streets yelled, "Balek, balek!" in an attempt to secure a space. The impoverished murmured, "Allah yjib..."May Allah provide.

Additionally, there was an abundance of destitution. True destitution is not comprehended until one observes the impoverished in Muslim countries.

The Jemaa el-Fna was bustling with activity, with petitioners in rags, vendors, snake charmers, and storytellers all congregating under the sun. The air was permeated with the aroma of fried food, cinnamon, mint, and unusual concoctions. The skulls of their clients were positioned over brass dishes by open-air barbers, who were able to administer bloodletting while conversing.

In that vast square, clandestine documents were discreetly transferred beneath burnooses on a daily basis.

Following that, we would saunter into the souk.

The merchants recognized me as they called out from their diminutive stalls. Children with wide-eyed expressions cried out, "S'phine, S'phine!" I donned the attire of a Muslim woman, but I refrained from wearing a hijab over my mouth. Initially, the Arabs murmured, but they soon began referring to me as "Little Sister." Occasionally, I engaged in heated arguments with them regarding their treatment of animals. They had been reared in a harsh manner themselves, which I comprehended.

Initially, I resided at the La Mamounia Hotel. Subsequently, I desired to reside in my own residence, as they did. I discovered a residence in the Medina, concealed at the terminus of a narrow passage. Before my servant, who was attired in white, could unlock the diminutive wooden door, visitors struck it three times.

The interior was a sanctuary, featuring blue mosaic corridors, a courtyard illuminated by natural light, and orange trees that consistently produced fruit. The fountain served as a drinkable source for birds. Shadows extended across marble pillars. The muezzin's summons to prayer reverberated through the air five times daily: "La illaha illa

Allah..."

I was subsequently invited to Si Mohamed Menebhi's residence. He would become yet another distinguished advocate for France's cause. His daughters—Fela, Rafet, and Hagdousch—became cherished to me. We both donned plush woolen jellabs.

I continue to hold dear a composition that bears the name of his wife:

When the evening stars vanish, When visions embark on their journey in the morning

As the sun rises, Does love also depart? Dark emissary, I am sorry!

His devoted servants—Aïcha, Lamber, and Ourika—welcomed me as one of their own.

Allow me to remain in Marrakesh for an additional period of time prior to my illness. The snowy peaks of the Atlas Mountains shone above the palm plantations in the autumn and spring. The trees were interconnected by streams that resembled silver streamers.

Moulay Larbi, our friend, carried news from Tétouan one evening: the possibility of a Spanish and German attack on Morocco was imminent.

What methods would we employ to acquire additional information?

I was in Casablanca the following day. The following day, Tangier. Next, I embarked on a three-week tour of Spain. I attended every embassy invitation and gathering in Barcelona and Madrid, where information was exchanged.

I returned to Morocco with a plethora of messages and concealed notes, even within my attire.

I visited a physician in Casablanca. The bronchitis I had contracted in Marseille had persisted for an excessively extended period. Additionally, I was in a state of agitation regarding whether or not it was feasible for me to bear children. That had become my preoccupation.

I underwent an examination by a specialist.

A few days later, in Marrakesh, I was lying in bed with a fever, pulverized ice pressing against my abdomen. The diagnosis: an infection that was the result of the radiologist's injection. Potential for peritonitis.

Jack was frightened. I was evacuated from Casablanca that evening. I observed my colleagues' dread, despite the fact that they are typically so brave. They attempted to smile.

There you have it. They administered anesthesia to me.

Dr. Comte was the operator. He rescued me.

However, I remained at the institution for nineteen months, from June 1941 to December 1942.

The pace of life in a hospital bed, where one inhales the odor of ether, is excruciatingly sluggish. My animals were my desire; I desired to converse with them and convey information that only animals could comprehend.

I recalled Gigolo, my diminutive African sparrow, who had passed away the previous winter. His tiny feet curled toward the sky, and I discovered him motionless in his cage.

Rather, I gazed at the ceiling's altering shadows. I awaited.

However, even misfortune has its advantages. My hospital room in Casablanca was transformed into an intelligence hub—a secure, tranquil gathering place for men who were strategizing for the future.

If only you had observed my legs! In a mere three weeks, they decayed. The first time I stood up, I concealed them beneath a long yellow dress. However, I was abruptly unable to walk. A dancer who was unable to stand—oh, là là! I was required to relearn, putting one foot in front of the other, with the assistance of aides. Nevertheless, I continued to visit the other patients, assuring them that they would also recover: "You will also recover..." There is no need for concern.

I was under the impression that I was more sturdy than I actually was. I accepted an invitation to Rabat in the hopes that the tranquil Oudaya Gardens would facilitate my recuperation. However, news of the United States' declaration of war on Germany reached three days later. I was ecstatic... Subsequently, a fever ensued. Peritonitis has recurred. Additional regimens, needles, and sulfonamides. The following words were added to my vocabulary: tachycardia, relapse, and lapse. "Dr. Bolot was not pleased." Neither was I.

1941 Christmas. Tiny candles flickered on a tree in a corner of my room. I have always had a fondness for Christmas; the joy of children reminds me of my own boyhood in St. Louis, where I cleared snow to earn a few cents for gifts. Every child, particularly the most impoverished, is entitled to joy during the Christmas season.

However, I was not in a position to exult. Dr. Comte introduced me to a new term: septicemia. "A probability of one in five..." Additionally, there is an additional term that is concerning: intestinal obstruction. Exactly what I required! And then Jack arrived—my guardian angel. We prayed.

A tapping at the window sounded one morning in spring '42, accompanied by thousands of small taps. Locusts! The sky was engulfed by a multitude of black and yellow insects. I endeavored to domesticate one. It was crushed by the caregiver.

"Well, Miss Nurse, you are an elderly locust yourself!"

I read history books during the periods when the injections were not too painful. Next, at nine o'clock in the morning on June 28, 1942, I was transported to surgery once more. What an extraordinary way to commence the day! An intolerable thirst and a thick, heavy tongue. I consumed alcohol for eight days. Subsequently, I experienced hunger.

However, the situation was exceedingly favorable. Embolism. Dammit!

I was fortunate to be rescued by Mademoiselle Marie Rochas.

After that, Saki arrived. I had heard his diminutive meows, but I was so drowsy from surgery that I believed I was hallucinating. A kitten—frail, scruffy, and scarcely larger than a rat. From what location had he arrived? The clinic prohibited the presence of animals.

"Bring that cat to me."

He was now under my ownership. Saki was the name I gave to him, although others referred to him as Fleabag. He preferred it more. I knitted him a small cardigan.

„Hello, Saki?"

He opened his eyes, revealing his diminutive tongue. He was perpetually attentive. I nursed him back to health. Love is a universal healer, whether it is directed toward humans or creatures.

Saki's frantic screams woke me up on November 8, 1942. Bombs were detonated throughout the vicinity. The Americans had arrived. I hastily retrieved my robe and proceeded to the terrace of the clinic. We witnessed the unfolding of history for three days and nights.

On November 11, American and French troops marched in unison through Casablanca. Tears streamed down my face as I stood at attention. I desired to embrace each combatant.

I was a soldier; however, Soldier Baker's mission had concluded. I believed that was the case. I was still too feeble to participate in combat, which caused me an indescribable amount of frustration.

I returned to Marrakesh on December 1 with the intention of spending Christmas with my friends and children.

However, Destiny had other ideas.

I was confined to my bed with typhoid fever during the Christmas season. Once more.

What actions could I take? Have you reached your limit? May I allow myself to perish? Oh, no.

I relocated to Si Menebhi's palace, a tranquil haven, immediately after my fever subsided. I was depressed. However, it is imperative to maintain happiness whenever one is dissatisfied. You are required to perform.

Even if you are trembling like a leaf.

Despite the fact that your abdomen has been sliced open.

No, mine did not recover. However, I was the one in command, not my body. I was back in Casablanca by February, inaugurating the Liberty Club for Black American soldiers, despite the advice of Jack and the doctor.

I performed three tracks. After that, I attempted to perform. However, my cranium was in a state of disarray, my stomach was burning, and stars were flashing before my eyes.

Handheld mine.

Miss Baker, I implore you to...

I sat up with my back erect.

"General, I am at your disposal!"

On that evening, General Clark, Patton, Anderson, Alexander, and Cunningham received me at the Anfa Hotel. However, what is the most surprising aspect? The General himself flew in Moulay Larbi and Si Menebhi.

I resumed my career as an artist.

I provided the Allied soldiers with my music, my joy, and my songs on the condition that I would not receive payment. I sang for my fellow soldiers, not for financial gain.

Allow them to coordinate transportation. Allow them to provide us with sustenance as required. However, there is no financial backing.

I did not receive a single franc until the conclusion of the conflict. It was not self-righteousness. It was entirely appropriate. I had debts to pay, while the Free French had so little.

I was loaned to the Americans and then the British by the Français Libres, but I continued to serve France exclusively. I observed the power struggles that were occurring behind the scenes as a result of my intelligence work. I issued a warning to each of them:

"I am willing to participate if it is beneficial to France." We are enemies if we do not.

There was a cost associated with that posture. Moldy bread and canned food of suspect quality were endured by me. No remorse.

I performed for the Black American troops under Colonel Wyatt, the white American troops under Colonel Meyer (General Eisenhower's colleague), and subsequently for Major Dunstan of the British ENSA. However, I ultimately remained with the Free French, despite the internal conflicts.

My tour organizer was Fernand Zimmer, who was previously employed as a foreign trade adviser. Unbelievably courageous.

Fred Rey, my former dancer at Casino de Paris, joined us as well. He was born in Austria and enlisted in the French Foreign Legion in 1939. However, he was incarcerated in a camp during the assaults. Jack was obligated to extract him.

I was treated to a farewell celebration at Si Menebhi's palace by my Marrakesh friends prior to my initial tour with the Americans, which was reminiscent of a scene from One Thousand and One Nights.

Moroccans in burnooses, Frenchmen, and Americans—both black and white—congregated in the courtyard beneath vines that were laden with blood-red blossoms. Between marble columns, Arabic music wafted.

It was here that I first witnessed the Blue Dance of the mountain people. Colonel Archie Roosevelt, the son of the U.S. President, observed the spectacle unfurl in the illuminated hall beyond the fountain, where water lilies floated.

My initial performances were held at the Rialto cinema in Casablanca, with the purpose of raising funds for the Red Cross. The stage was occupied by Spahis in full uniform, their swords drawn.

I concluded the performance with J'ai Deux Amours. The room was jolted by the acclaim. There was only one passion that night—the one we all shared: Paris.

I sang three to four times a day for a month, between Oran and Algiers, occasionally on makeshift stages consisting of tin cans and timber planks. It is irrelevant. Tents were the location of my costume modifications. They adored my final anthem, my Brazilian scarf, my Breton clogs, and my dress in the hues of Paris.

I was accompanied by a small volunteer orchestra, which consisted of Black soldiers using instruments to provide their music.

I observed fireworks in the sky while dressed as a cabaret performer near Oran one evening. Then, darkness ensued. The spotlights of the truck are turned off. The audience collapsed to the ground. Likewise, I did.

We were being dive-bombed by German aircraft.

In order to divert my attention, I held onto my sandwich. This was followed by a voice emanating from the darkness:

"Miss Baker?" "Miss Baker?"

A soldier crept toward me.

He was delivering vanilla ice cream to me.

After taking a break in Marrakesh in the spring of 1943, I encountered General de Gaulle's aides in Algiers. The Free French were confronted with retaliation, politics, and obstacles.

Instead of singing for our troops in Gabès and Tripoli, I was dispatched to accompany the British. In a mere three weeks, my English proficiency enabled us to traverse Egypt and the Near East.

I performed at army barracks, airfields, and hospitals that were crowded with wounded soldiers from El Alamein and Bir Hakeim. I was greeted cordially by the French ambassador in Beirut, but I could sense that there was trouble. The Atlantic Charter had been effectively memorized by the Muslims; however, there were murmurs that suggested otherwise.

I returned on July 15. I forewarned my companions. They implemented an action plan.

I embarked on a new tour this time, this time in support of the Free French Resistance.

And that, Monsieur Sauvage, was only the beginning.

The desert is not devoid of life; it is enigmatic and vibrant. Mirages appear as hauntingly beautiful sirens from the past, and the wind speaks, rumbling like a drum.

We slept on the ground at night, with one of us constantly on guard, our coats tightly coiled. Figures were observed scavenging wreckage and snatching from the deceased as shadows moved. In the midst of ruined tanks, broken planes, and burnt-out automobiles, jackals and hyenas were observed sniffing out bodies.

Alexandria was our destination for four days.

Prince Mohamed Ali addressed France's involvement in the Middle East.

"The Arab nations must be guided by France." Independence is desirable, but it is only achievable when one is genuinely prepared for it. We require stability, certainty, and leadership in the Arab world, which is currently unstable.

Our arrangements were established in Cairo; however, we were compelled to expedite our journey to Beirut. There, I sold my diminutive gold Cross of Lorraine at auction, raising 350,000 francs for the Resistance.

From Beirut to Damascus, and then to Jerusalem, the King David Hotel twinkled in marble under the miraculous light. All was evident—everything was crisp and visible.

Si Mohamed Menebhi and Jack conversed with the Arabs in Jericho and beyond. However, Arab Union slogans that were endorsed by the British were rapidly disseminating.

Anti-French demonstrations had erupted in Cairo by the time we returned to Judaea. We nevertheless performed, and King Peter of Yugoslavia and King Farouk were present in the audience.

We returned to Algiers on November 15, 1943, after traversing the Sahara. The temperature was frigid. The sole backdrop I had ever required was the Cross of Lorraine flag, which had been meticulously hand-stitched by nuns. I lowered my cap and enveloped myself in it.

The conclusion of each year had been unkind for a period of three years.

Another surgical procedure was performed in December 1943. I was once again in Marrakesh Hospital in January 1944, scarcely managing to maintain my life.

Nevertheless, my companions remained. And so did the prayers of three hundred impoverished, blind, and disabled individuals who had been provided with sustenance by Si Mohamed Menebhi. They were now kneeling beneath my window, praying for my recovery.

I was able to recuperate.

I resumed performing in April at the request of General Béthouart for a celebration in Algiers that was dedicated to the air force.

I resulted in the French Air Force incurring an aircraft expense.

General Bouscat, who had facilitated my promotion to second lieutenant, dispatched me to Morocco on a Seagull. We were compelled to return to Meknes due to a tempest. The initial warning.

A second Seagull was awaiting at Boufarik. The Allies entered Bayeux that morning. The wind was brimming with pleasure, and the sky was pristine. Zimmer, Jack, René Guérin, and I embarked on a journey to Corsica.

Sunlight illuminated the cabin, rendering it golden. Kabylia's mountains were dispersed beneath them like flocks of livestock. Subsequently, the unrestricted sea.

One engine experienced a deceleration.

"Please wait... it is ceasing."

The left engine malfunctioned.

"The pilot is confident that the other individual will be able to handle the situation."

A massive granite wall loomed ahead, suggesting that Corsica was imminent.

Zimmer murmured, "We will never be able to resolve it."

Choking occurred in the turbine. The aircraft initiated a pitch. We prepared for the potential impact.

We managed to leap over the mountain, only to promptly plummet toward the water. The captain yelled:

"Brace yourselves!"

Shock. A accident that exceeded the threshold of hearing. A burst of white water.

Colored riflemen, who were bathing and were unclothed, rushed onto the shore. They navigated the water with the grace of seals. They rescued us.

Another aircraft was dispatched by General Bouscat.

"If it's a Seagull," I communicated, "I'm not getting on."

It was a Glenn Martin. Our initial directive is to arrive in Cagliari.

The night before a significant battle, I sang one final time before returning to France. I was surrounded by aircraft that were glinting in the moonlight, as I stood by a mast that was adorned with the Cross of Lorraine.

Four years of separation from France.

I requested to be repatriated immediately upon Marseille's liberation. With my compatriots, I desired to serve in France.

I was assigned to the initial roster.

A convent located near Algiers was the location where all of the air force females convened. From there, we were transported to Mers El-Kébir by a military train, where we alighted onto a Liberty Ship.

An officer conducted an inspection of us at the pier.

"No animals allowed on board."

"But what about Mitraillette?"

Mitraillette, the mascot of our unit, was a diminutive dog that I had chosen for his propensity to urinate in brief, sharp bursts, as evidenced by his appellation, "rat-tat-tat."

I had already lost all of my livestock in Africa. I was determined not to lose him as well.

He was smuggled from bag to bag until a storeroom worker admitted him.

As a result, Mitraillette and I found ourselves in Marseille.

9

SECRETS FROM THE BOUDOIR

Jo and Jo

Monsieur Sauvage, I am not fond of that title or the term "boudoir." Pretentious and artificial, it leaves a stale residue. And if you anticipate that I will address my preferences for males, my fascination with beauty marks, or the techniques that intrigue me, you will be left waiting indefinitely.

I would never sell my memories, particularly the personal ones, to regain the prominence, even if I were impoverished. Some artists are unable to compose their own narratives, resulting in tales that are neither elegant, fascinating, nor decent.

People claim that I still possess the spirit of a young, African American lady. Potentially. Presently, they accuse me of concealing my identity. No problem. I will be unassuming, akin to a small savage. The sole personal treasure of life is modesty; otherwise, it is merely an additional source of sorrow to the world's suffering.

Confidential information? I retain them.

In other words, I have always been in love. An artist who lacks passion, seduction, or faith in the enigma of love is not an artist at all. Art is the pursuit of beauty, passion, and seduction. My mother was my initial passion. Afterward, my father. Then, my brother, who operates a garage in St. Louis.

Until 1949, my mother had never witnessed me perform. She was so overcome that her nose bled through the entirety of the Folies show. She sat there, cotton balls lodged in her nostrils, unable to comprehend that I was indeed her daughter. However, I had a residence in Dordogne, near Les Milandes, that was prepared for her. She and my sister had their perfectly healthy teeth extracted in preparation for the transition to a new set of fashionable artificial teeth. These teeth featured blue gums, as was the custom for non-white individuals in the United States. They aimed to awe the French. Regrettably, Mama's new molars caused her discomfort. She was devastated; she was unable to giggle as much as she desired. However, she is currently content with our relationship.

The first person I fell in love with as a child was a young white lad who was a redhead with freckles everywhere. I was astounded. I was too timid to speak, so I simply gazed at him, shifting my eyes so violently that I must have alarmed him.

I intentionally placed my photograph in front of him one day in the expectation that he would engage in conversation. He retrieved it and stated, "You may keep it." I fled out of humiliation.

Subsequently, we engaged in recreation. I suggested to him, "Let's pretend we are in love!" I buried my head between my shoulders as he caressed my hair. "You are the most beautiful girl in the world," he declared. I wept with joy.

He never touched me. He was inadequately proportioned. However, I adored him—oh, how I adored him!

It is possible that it is a dream or a film narrative that I have conflated with my own. Upon reflection, life is akin to a collection of film images that are often unexpected and appear to belong to someone else. Some memories remain vivid, while others recede into mute shadows.

Pepito Abatino, my manager from 1926 to 1935, was a diplomat with the charm of a diplomat and a slender, refined build. He was Italian and was known for his unrelenting work ethic, which may have been excessive. He advocated for me when I was uncertain about how to manage contracts, documents, or the traps concealed behind smiling features and chocolate boxes that were larger than suitcases.

For nine years, he dedicated himself to my professional pursuits, sharing my aspirations for the opportunities that life could offer. He even envisioned me as a novelist. He composed Mon Sang dans Tes Veines (My Blood in Your Veins) under my name after I recounted tales about white and colored individuals in America. The preface was composed by me.

The novel recounts the life of Joan, a diminutive black girl who, like many of my acquaintances in St. Louis, was of African descent. We would flee the Louisiana humidity by the river, observing the coal-covered longshoremen regain their whiteness after a swim. "Do you see?" In any case, what makes a color? Joan would say.

I desired the book to present an alternative perspective on the defense of children of color. Joan was intelligent, tormented, and akin to a small avian that was covered in coal dust, unable to comprehend why people looked down on her.

At that time, I provided her with comfort. The tri-colored blood of my family—Mama was colored, Papa was European, and Aunt Elvira was Indian—cleared my understanding. Mon Sang dans Tes Veines is a play that explores the implicit drama of mixed blood in America, specifically a blood transfusion.

Joan and I discovered a colored Virgin Mary in an abandoned chapel at one time. It was a revelation to us—a sign that we were seen, adored, and protected.

Joan... What happened to her?

I was married to white males.

Poor Pepito succumbed to a gastrointestinal ulcer. His funeral was held at Saint Philippe du Roule in Paris. I now desire for him to be interred in close proximity to me, at Château des Milandes, adjacent to the small chapel where my most recent matrimony was sanctified. Pepito, I have known you since my childhood.

Jean Lion, a young Jewish industrialist, married me in Crèvecoeur-le-Grand in 1936. The law was read to us by the mayor, Monsieur Jammy Schmidt, who then delivered a charming speech. Jean was overjoyed. Likewise, I was.

However, we parted ways after three years and divorced shortly thereafter. The judge summarized the situation as follows: "A couple who have never sighted each other." He was correct.

Jean departed for work an hour after I arrived home at dawn. The afternoon was spent in slumber. I was compelled to perform by the evening, frequently before Jean returned. This was not an appropriate way to live.

The audience is the actual family of an artist.

However, Jean's mother continues to be known as Mama Lion to me. She always greeted me with warmth and asserted that I was the sole woman capable of managing her son. Regrettably, I am unable to assert that he was the sole individual capable of managing me in the manner that my profession necessitates.

We maintained our friendship. Jean even requested that I marry him again following our divorce. However, life had other intentions.

Divorce was never my intention; however, I am not susceptible to delusions.

I assisted Jean and his family in obtaining documents to enable them to escape to Brazil during the occupation.

After Paris was liberated, I encountered Jo Bouillon at the Théâtre aux Armées upon my return to France. He was conducting at Le Boeuf sur le Toit.

He generously accompanied me. While racing between posts behind the Armée de la Victoire, we performed for soldiers in harsh conditions, fostering a close bond. Our love was born in the ruins, to the melodies of violins, on improvised stages.

Subsequently, he abdicated a portion of his professional career in favor of mine.

My birthday, June 3, 1947, was the date on which we were married at Château des Milandes.

That was an extraordinary ceremony!

The petals that covered the path from the château to the chapel were protected by local children in order to preserve them prior to the ceremony.

However, there is no organ.

Jo conducted a survey of the countryside at dawn and discovered a harmonium in Domme. The 80-year-old parish vicar desired to lend it, but he was unable to do so due to transportation constraints.

The village butcher intervened.

Our harmonium was transported to the sanctuary by an enormous truck, the same one that the Germans employed to remove statues from Paris.

We had our soundtrack.

A unique violin composition was performed by Jo's sibling.

In accordance with custom, the locals served pepper soup to the newlywed that evening in order to provide him with warmth.

Jo consumed every morsel.

We departed for the United States five days later.

I encountered a few of de Gaulle's officers prior to my departure. I informed them of the following:

"Is there not something more significant than politics?" Wouldn't the release of Marshal Pétain provide an opportunity to reconcile all individuals of goodwill?

A number of individuals concurred. However, others declined—with an excessive degree of determination.

I departed.

I will provide you with information about America at a later time.

But first, the charming narrative of Jo and me prior to our marriage.

I promptly visited General Chadebec de Lavalade, the commander of the Fifteenth Military Region, upon my arrival in Marseille in 1944 with Mitraillette.

The Théâtre des Armées was no longer in existence. Casualties were in dire need of assistance, yet no service was available to provide it.

I was assigned the responsibility of assembling a troupe by the general.

I required an orchestra. Jo Bouillon was recommended by Yves Bonnat, who was in the process of purging music halls of suspected collaborators.

Paris had been liberated for a few weeks. Jo was performing at Le Boeuf sur le Toit.

I left him a note indicating that we had an essential meeting scheduled for 2 a.m. at my residence.

Jo roused me at 2 a.m.

I greeted him in a 36-layer turban, which is my customary attire for sleeping warm. He was taken aback.

I submitted my proposal: I would relinquish all responsibilities, including compensation and a timetable.

His pupils expanded.

I elaborated for an hour.

Afterward, he entered.

We made our début in Marseille for war victims eight days later, accompanied by twenty-five musicians. Two million francs were raised during the tour.

Consequently, Jo and I initiated our relationship.

We collaborated with the First Army, particularly those deployed to the African commando units, and followed closely behind. I possessed a permanent military mission order and diplomatic safe-conducts. We performed along the way, occasionally in a barn illuminated by oil lamps or by the roadside with only a guitar. The group was consistently united by Jo, who maintained a positive attitude. The musicians were located in one location, Jo in another, and I was with the officers. Rations were in short supply; some soldiers even relinquished theirs to us. We sang for them, regardless of whether it was snowing or muddy.

Who would have refrained from adhering to Colonel Bouvet?

Upon our arrival during the liberation of Alsace, Belfort was enveloped in snow. I requested permission to proceed to the front line, which is situated at a bridgehead twenty kilometers distant. Major Ferragi transported me in a jeep, and we subsequently proceeded on foot, traversing the snow in small groups amid the exploding projectiles.

We and the Resistance reopened theaters in every city, including Mulhouse, Nancy, and Colmar, as the army advanced. We continued to perform in Strasbourg as the Germans unleashed counterattacks. Additionally, we participated in the initial crossing of the Rhine. Upon the commando soldiers' return from a deep incursion into German lines, we presented them with a unique performance.

I pursued Senegalese personnel in every location. Many of them sustained severe frostbite on their feet. One day, in the highlands beyond Konstanz, one of them presented me with a baby deer. It was his final cherished possession. I was hesitant to accept it, but he persisted, his eyes welling with tears.

We arrived in Berlin on January 3, 1945, for the inaugural gala of the Allies, which was attended by four generals. Four groups of artists—British, French, Russian, and American—performed. I was privileged to represent France alongside Jo Bouillon and Colette Mars, a dear friend, the daughter of General Huot, and a relative of the Bishop of Algiers.

The gala was held in the courthouse, which was surrounded by rats and debris. Berlin was entirely unrecognizable—there were no avenues, parks, or monuments—only craters, debris, and skeletal iron beams.

In the interior, four extravagant banquets remained unattended. The American guards' white gloves appeared to be on fire as the brilliant stage lights reflected off them during the intermissions. The performance was concluded by me. Jo and his musicians were exceptional. The applause was overwhelming, but I reassured myself: "No, Josephine, they're not applauding for you, but for France—the country that, twenty years ago, embraced a little colored dancer who only wanted to escape, to do well, to always do better, if luck allowed."

We remained in Berlin for a period of ten days. The generals' gala had concluded; however, what about the soldiers?

We located a small cinema in the French quarter and performed non-stop from ten in the morning until eleven at night for them—the ones who genuinely deserved it. A fresh show is broadcast every two hours. The orchestra operated continuously. Jo continued to propel herself forward like a windmill. Soldiers could attend for a mere two cents. In exchange, they presented us with mountains of German Aryan certificates, which they had discovered in the basement of the Reichstag, weighing hundreds of kilograms. Evidence that we would remain "good Aryans" indefinitely!

"And my domestic helper?" I assure you that the former Chief of Police of Potsdam was a most exquisite butler.

We traversed cities that were devastated, including Karlsruhe, Stuttgart, and Hamburg. In Hamburg, there were kilometers of debris, resembling a desert. In silence, thousands of bells, which had been stolen from various locations throughout Europe, rested along the docks. These bells had previously tolled for the Angelus in far-off villages.

General de Monsabert, a man of African descent, greeted me in Sigmaringen. He was a man who was revered and respected by all. He was accompanied by a Goumier honor escort. I was seated to his right in the magnificent reception hall of the château, which was a marble trophy room belonging to the Hohenzollern family. It is possible that I was the first Black woman to stand in that location, which was once the gathering place for males who ruthlessly formulated Hitler's racial policies. In the presence of five generals, I stood there, feeling both humble and proud.

At night, I retired to a diminutive icy chalet that boasted an extraordinary panorama. Was it a dream? I continue to contemplate...

Afterward, tranquility ensued.

It was time to resume employment in order to reclaim the audience that existed prior to the war. I departed for Finland, in Scandinavia, where individuals believed that I had passed away. This allegation had been disseminated during my time in Moroccan hospitals. Throughout Europe, individuals harbored reservations regarding my credibility. The Swiss press engaged in a discussion regarding:

"It is not the genuine Josephine!" She has lost her figure; she is excessively emaciated.

Others disagreed:

"Her body may have changed, but her voice is unmistakable!"

The concept of mortality is readily accepted by individuals, while the living are more difficult to identify.

Every day, five hundred individuals assembled outside my hotel in Helsinki. My audiences were significantly different, ranging from the National Theater to the People's House, where I performed. I was so overwhelmed by the abundance of gifts that I made Finland a special place in my memory. In order to circumvent customs, I concealed six puppies beneath my outerwear upon my return. They were the progeny of a dog that a soldier had left at the French Consulate prior to his departure for war. I retained one—Flicka, which is currently located at Les Milandes, a sliver of Finland in the Dordogne.

Ultimately, Europe acknowledged my existence. I shifted my focus to Paris, where a significant number of individuals were still experiencing hardship. I personally visited Les Halles and La Villette to procure meat and vegetables for "Le pot-au-feu des vieux," a meal intended for the elderly. Unfortunately, the elderly and impoverished are frequently overlooked and neglected. In spite of all obstacles, no one takes sufficient measures to guarantee their survival.

My existence was characterized by turbulence in 1946. My marriage was precarious. Jo traveled to Switzerland, while I traveled to Morocco. In order to raise funds for the air force, I conducted my final mission in North Africa.

Upon my return, I was confined to Ambroise Paré Hospital, with the expectation that I would depart for the cemetery, as Raimu had done a few weeks prior. However, Jo arrived from Geneva and Jacques Abtey from Morocco to be by my bedside.

Doctors discontinued treatment at 2 a.m. However, affection and friendship are incompatible. They searched every pharmacy and hospital in quest of Subtosan, a rare medicine. I survived, despite the physicians' skepticism, as a result of a blood transfusion and that.

However, I did not recover.

In the autumn of 1946, I recuperated at Les Milandes, where I was surrounded by my animals and fields. I arrived in Paris on December 30. I was on the operating table for three and a half hours at Rue Georges Bizet the following morning. Subsequently, they informed me that they had examined my abdomen five times since 1940, but they were hesitant to handle anything. They were shaken by fear. They merely reconstructed me and left me to the mercy of God. It is possible that they were correct— Providence preserved my life for Dr. Thiroloix and Dr. Funck-Brentano, who ultimately restored my health.

"Dr. Thiroloix, I am grateful. "I am grateful, Dr. Funck-Brentano!" Although words are inadequate, nothing would ever be.

I was discharged from the hospital on January 21, 1947.

Jo and I had arranged our nuptials. I returned to Les Milandes.

Jo embarked on a journey to South America in March to coordinate our honeymoon tour. However, there were no contracts after six weeks. They continued to maintain the belief that I had either passed away or had aged by a hundred years in the span of ten years.

We were subsequently assisted by the renowned actor and singer, Hugo del Carril.

Jo and Jo were on their way to South America less than a week after our nuptials, an adventure that was characterized by turbulence.

Has America undergone a transformation?

I was under the impression that the United States had undergone a transformation. The conflict necessitated that white and colored soldiers engage in combat in tandem. Undoubtedly, this unity had contributed to the dismantling of racial barriers. I was anxious to observe the advancements firsthand after a twelve-year absence.

Jo and I had recently concluded an extensive tour of South America, during which we performed hundreds of performances. Our subsequent destination was Chicago, where we arrived via flight from Mexico. Our stay was uneventful. We felt secure enough to request that our associates reserve an apartment at a prestigious New York hotel under the name Mr. and Mrs. Jo Bouillon.

The Secret Walls of New York

Reality struck immediately upon our arrival in New York.

"You can stay, but..."

Jo was contacted by the hotel manager shortly after we had settled in.

"How long do you plan to stay, Mr. Bouillon?"

"A month," Jo replied.

"I apologize for the error." Your apartment is exclusively accessible for the evening. It has been reserved for tomorrow.

Jo comprehended the situation immediately.

"Is this because my wife is colored?"

The manager hesitated.

There was a spoken phrase.

Although colored individuals were legally equal, they were not regarded as such, particularly in New York, where the social norms were still established by wealthy Southern guests. No hotel was willing to jeopardize their business by accommodating a mixed couple, regardless of whether they were legally married.

We encountered the same response at each hotel.

"No rooms for colored women!" was an outright statement that no one ventured to make. That would constitute an unlawful act. Rather, they offered apologies, which were consistently polite and characterized by a sincere "sorry."

We were able to reserve accommodations at the Gladstone Hotel on Park Avenue. Three days transpired without incident. Subsequently, the spectacle resumed.

"Mr. Bouillon, I apologize deeply." Your accommodations have been reserved by another individual for tomorrow.

Jo declined to depart this time.

In the interim, we had disclosed our ordeal to Canada Lee, the renowned Black actor on Broadway. Canada Lee, similar to Lena Horne and other Black celebrities, was permitted to reside in New York, provided that they maintained their residence. He assured us that he would advocate for us.

He immediately approached Mayor O'Dwyer, who provided him with the following assurance:

"Please inform Mr. Bouillon and Miss Baker that the law is on their side." Please inform me if anyone attempts to compel them to leave, and I will take action.

Jo maintained her composure in the face of this assurance. The hotel did not request that we depart again; however, they rendered our stay intolerable.

Our dinner was delivered that evening without napkins, flatware, or plates.

I inquired, "What is the situation?"

"I apologize." We are experiencing a slight shortage of supplies.

The summon bell was disregarded.

The mattresses remained unmade the following day. The telephone malfunctioned.

It was plain to see: they would not compel us to leave; rather, they would drive us out.

At that instant, I made the decision to depart from the hotel and not only New York, but to proceed directly to the South. I was compelled to observe the conditions of my people in the Deep South, where segregation was still the law, if prejudice was still as severe in the North.

A Journey of Miss Brown

In order to unearth the truth, I was compelled to relinquish my identity as Josephine Baker, the French music hall star. Rather, I would embark on my journey as an ordinary Black woman, Miss Brown.

Jo was eager to attend.

I replied, "Certainly not." "A white individual would attract attention." Additionally, if they incarcerate me, someone must provide me with a bond.

"What if you sustain an injury?" What if they lynch you?

Jo was consistently the pessimist.

In order to alleviate his anxiety, I consented to allow Jeff Smith, a Black journalist, to accompany me. What is his position? To observe. He was not to intervene unless my life was truly in jeopardy.

Crossing the Mason-Dixon Line

Train reservations constitute our initial obstacle.

"Two sleepers for Nashville, please."

The agent briefly observed Jeff and Jo.

"For both of you?"

"Yes."

"Sorry, no space left."

The same occurred at numerous agencies.

"If we travel in regular seats," Jeff pointed out, "they'll force us into the colored car when we cross the Mason-Dixon Line."

Ultimately, Jeff deceived a travel agent into selling us two slumber tickets. We boarded the train at 9 p.m. the following evening.

Initially, the voyage was uneventful. Subsequently, we entered the dining compartment during lunchtime.

A maître d' arrived at our table in a hurry.

"I respectfully request that you expedite your actions." You have just enough time to complete the task before we reach the finish line.

"The line?"

The Mason-Dixon Line.

Four soldiers—three of whom were Caucasian and one of whom was Black—entered a few minutes later.

They were intercepted by the maître d'.

"I'm terribly sorry, but I can't serve you."

One of the white officers became enraged.

"Why?" We have recently endured the conflict as a unit; however, we are now unable to dine together.

The maître d' hesitated before lifting a drape.

"If you want to stay together… you'll have to sit here."

The "colored" section is situated behind it.

A new vehicle was incorporated at the subsequent halt. The sign read as follows:

"COLORED."

All Black passengers were directed to enter. Jeff and I were left alone, as our sleeper reservations provided us with protection. In the United States, a contract is a contract.

Segregation Testing

I elected to conduct an in-person examination of segregation laws during a one-hour intermission.

I instructed Jeff to remain on the train. "I'm going for a walk."

He cautioned, "Ensure that you do not receive an arrest."

Signs were ubiquitous outside:

"WHITE" – "COLORED."

Two bathrooms, two cafés, and two waiting spaces. Legally segregated.

I entered the café that was referred to as "white." Conversations were suspended. I was pursued by eyes.

"Two sandwiches and a kilo of apples, please."

The waitress hesitated before promptly presenting me with my order and accepting my payment.

I overheard a client mutter as I departed:

"Must be a stranger."

Then, I entered the café that was "colored."

I was greeted with sullen, nervous faces, anticipating approval. There was not a single smile of approval.

My gaze was greeted with warmth only by a stray, malnourished dog.

Jeff returned to the train and provided an explanation:

"You scared them."

"Because I bought apples in the white café?"

"Because you contested the regulations." "You are aware of the outcome if anyone had incited a fight."

He presented me with the Race Relations magazine. His apprehensions were validated by the headlines

BLOODSHED.

No charges have been filed against a Black man who was assaulted and shot by police in Kentucky.

A rent dispute resulted in the death of a Black war veteran in New York; no weapon was discovered on him.

A Black man in St. Louis was shot after allegedly stealing a comforter; the incident was deemed a "legal homicide."

Jeff was the subject of my gaze.

He inquired gently, "Do you comprehend now?"

Nashville and St. Louis

In Nashville, I once again assumed the role of Josephine Baker, delivering lectures to enthusiastic students. Their inquiries were delivered rapidly:

"Are there mixed marriages in France?"

"Would a white man let a Black doctor treat him?"

"Can a Black person get a top job?"

My responses astounded them.

One student had written to President Truman, requesting admission to a white graduate institution. Congress rendered a decision in her benefit. The first Black woman to attain that privilege, she walked away beaming.

I was reunited with my family in St. Louis. My sibling informed me that the Senate was currently discussing the issue of segregation in the military. Southern politicians expressed their intention to obstruct reforms by reading the Bible for days in a filibuster.

I returned to New York after visiting my family. This time, the lodgings failed to recognize that my apartment had been "reserved for someone else."

An Unpleasant Reality

I heard it in New York as well:

"No Jews, no dogs, no niggers."

The hypocrisy was particularly painful, particularly in the case of Jewish landlords in Harlem, who exploited Black tenants to a greater extent than white Americans.

Jews treated Harlem's Black community with the same cruelty they had once endured, despite the fact that the war had been fought against race policies.

I had witnessed injustice across nations, as I informed the Pope in Rome. However, what did I observe in the United States?

It had to be altered.

It is imperative that it be altered.

10

A FINAL WORD ON THE CELEBRITIES OF THE TIME

Impressions and Memories of Individuals I Have Interacted with

While I have encountered numerous celebrities, there are only a handful who are genuinely remarkable. I hold the highest regard for diligent labor, particularly when it is executed with enthusiasm. I am not intimidated by anyone. Ultimately, we all possess a head, a belly, two limbs, and two legs. That thought alone is sufficient to provide a sense of perspective. I prefer to observe rather than to render judgments. Life is already difficult enough without the addition of unwarranted criticism.

Although my companions on stage are exceptionally talented, my current focus is on comprehension rather than performance. The strongest individuals are those who maintain a youthful spirit. America instills in its citizens the virtues of vigor, courage, and agility, as well as the necessity of adapting to financial constraints. I yearn to remain eternally youthful, dancing and singing to my own beat, and living life at my own pace. It is possible that this will prove to be my undoing. However, if my body is exhausted during the procedure, so be it.

Despite being referred to as an imbecile by some, I continue to garner respect. I am not inclined to snobbery, and I have no tolerance for those who hold others in contempt. I am not in need of these stories, nor am I obligated to provide an explanation to anyone as a result of the preposterous ones that have been told about me. God is present within me. He is the source of my liberation and fortitude. I dedicate my time to the pursuit of life.

However, I am able to provide a few impressions—brief illustrations, mere glimpses. I am circumspect, despite my own nature, so there is nothing definitive to say.

Diplomacy and flattery

An exhausting game—diplomacy, discretion, and appearances! If I were to disclose even a small portion of the knowledge and experiences I have encountered... Ah là là! Josephine's life would be terminated. Perhaps the truth will be recorded at some point. We must all work, live, and participate in the game until that time. Monsieur Sauvage, it is important to remember that individuals only seek flattery. Charm and delusion are the primary mechanisms by which relationships are sustained.

Therefore, let us concentrate on those whom we cherish.

Vincent Auriol: The Citizen President

In 1948, I encountered Vincent Auriol at the Colonial Exhibition. He approached my booth and extended a cordial welcome:

"Bonjour, Monsieur le Président."

His smile was adorned with a fatherly tenderness, and he spoke with a gentle accent. He epitomizes the ideal of a citizen president—chubby, genial, and likable—while remaining straightforward and approachable. He is responsible for that, after all.

A Monarch with Grace: King Gustaf of Sweden

The humble monarch. He extended an invitation to me to join his family and reside in his residence. We reconnected in France when he traveled through Paris on his way to play tennis in the South.

He exudes a delicate radiance and a certain grace, which the Moroccans refer to as barakah. People are apprehensive about his vulnerability, not out of obligation, but out of affection. He is admired for his ability to remain in the background while still commanding respect from others. The Swedish populace holds him in high regard, as he is an elderly monarch who is responsible for the protection of a youthful and prosperous nation. May he and his nation continue to be resilient.

Elevating Our Art: Katherine Dunham

Katherine Dunham is distinct from conventional Negro art. Three times, I attended her performance, and each time, I was more enraptured.

She is tall, elegant, and incredibly educated. Her irises gleam like those of an Egyptian statue, and her hands move with the precision of a scholar. I introduced her to French radio because I am enthusiastic about any endeavor that promotes the advancement of our race.

Her dancers would be perceived as equals to the Ballets Russes if they were not Black but wore a distinct style of dress. This is not merely a stylized performance; it is a refined, elevated art form. There is no trace of primitiveness. It challenges outmoded perceptions and demonstrates our capabilities.

Katherine, our beloved Katherine, is already phenomenal.

The Strict Gentleman: General Clark

A man who never quips, yet is quite amusing—a strict general with the demeanor of a gentleman. He is tall, pure, and meticulously dressed, resembling a Philadelphia catalogue model.

Firm, yet refined and considerate. He commands; he does not obey.

Luigi Pirandello: My Uncle of Words

I used to refer to him as my uncle, Luigi Pirandello. He frequently visited me in Le Vésinet or perched in a box at the Casino. He found it to be quite enjoyable.

A tiny, bearded man with a sharp goatee that is perpetually in motion, and eyes that are brimming with restless energy. He was endearing but restless, akin to a headstrong Sicilian goat.

He once entertained the notion of composing a play for me and even initiated the process. He would flit from subject to subject, laughing with the carefree joy of a child discovering new grass. He would then become softer and more empathetic.

A Soulmate in Letters: Colette

Oh, Colette! I discovered a sibling in her, an individual who shares my affection for plants, flowers, and animals.

She communicates with me on paper that is delicate, such as white, pink, blue, ivory, or Japanese paper. I preserve her letters as talismans.

Her voice possesses a profundity that establishes a connection with reality. You are grounded by her. One is incapable of floating away.

Additionally, her irises! They caress everything they see, their eyes dark and replete.

And her tresses! In contrast to mine, it is smoky, open, and evaporative. Mine adheres to me.

She is generous and comprehends the music venue. Everywhere she has been, she has been behind the scenes.

"Colette—I adore her!"

The Greek Prince and Princess: Royal in Spirit

In Beirut, I encountered Peter of Greece and his princess. We have maintained a close friendship.

They are attractive not only in terms of their physical appearance, but also in their spirituality. Their nobility is genuine; it is not ceremonial.

They are intelligent, engaged, and interested in all forms of art, and they move with an effortless elegance. They observe and listen with dignity.

They do not merely observe; they participate. These individuals are even more extraordinary than words can convey due to their generosity.

Maurice Dekobra: The Jungle Gentleman

Examine the text he composed for me:

"In remembrance of the Parisian jungle, Josephine Baker, my fairy of the tropics and the unforgettable creator of the Siren." With warmest regards.

He perceives Paris as a wilderness. It is possible that he is correct.

We shared our experiences during the filming process, despite the fact that one scenario was extremely costly. Rolling in powder! A catastrophe. We can now chuckle about it.

Monsieur Sauvage, you are claiming that you observed him on the beaches of Southern France, clad in checkered shirts and a bandana, as if he were a music hall cowboy. I have never done so.

A refined and poised international gentleman, he was always to me. His visage, which is characterized by sharp ridges and straight lines, is indicative of his discipline. However, there is a benevolence that lies beneath it.

Concluding thoughts

My fascination with individuals is not based on their fame, but rather on the underlying qualities that captivate me. A few captivate me with their charm, while others impress me with their fortitude, and others endear me with their sincerity.

Their public identities remain intact as numerous individuals fulfill their roles. Only a small number of individuals disclose their authentic selves.

It is possible that the complete truth will be revealed at some point. I will persist in living, observing, and—when feasible—dancing to my own beat until that time.

Reflections and Interactions

The Sons of Power: Spoiled Yet Appealing

The Negus's son is a friend—certainly a commendable one—but he is a pampered child, as are so many others. Another example is Archie Roosevelt, the son of the president. Intelligent, carefree, and at ease in all environments. His skin becomes translucent, resembling a crimson balloon, as a result of his insistence on drinking straight. Handle with caution; sensitive. However, they are exceedingly benevolent.

Moroccan Nobility: Visionaries for Change

His Majesty Moulay Larbi el Alaoui, the cousin of the Sultan of Morocco, and His Excellency Mohamed Menebhi have accomplished more for Morocco and will continue to do so for all Muslim women in Africa than many are aware.

Moulay Larbi is a colossus in both stature and presence, with a heart that is equally impressive. He is a genuine statesman, refined, and modern. I have encountered numerous individuals and am capable of making assessments. He speaks with a combination of courtesy and wisdom.

In Morocco, males are genuinely adept at maintaining a mustache, as evidenced by the solid and imposing appearance of Mohamed

Menebhi, whose eyes were ablaze with black fire beneath his sharp mustache. Rightfully, he was awarded the Legion of Honor in 1949. He and Moulay Larbi collaborate to advance Moroccan women's rights, which have already been achieved by their Egyptian and Turkish counterparts. That is not a simple task. Nevertheless, they will obtain success.

The Charmer of Politics: President Herriot

I am impressed by President Herriot's humanity, sincerity, and knowledge, which are uncommon qualities in politicians. He possesses a talent for engaging with the most significant debates as if they had just occurred to him. His manners are persuasive without being overbearing, and his laughter is both welcoming and boisterous. A man whose expertise is captivating rather than intimidating. Was there another individual of this nature? Monnerville, the president.

However, let us return to Africa.

Georges Duhamel: A Man of Music and Words

At our meeting in Buenos Aires, he informed me, "Maestro, your voice is reminiscent of a turtledove."

He is a wordsmith who effortlessly envelops you, his hands facilitating each conversation. Even though his criticisms are gentle, they are highly effective.

Jo and Gabriel Bouillon performed Bach's Double Violin Concerto for him at the French embassy one evening. He closed his eyes as he absorbed the melody. He harbors an abhorrence for the disorderly nature of contemporary American dance.

King Farouk: A Ruler Admired by His People

I encountered King Farouk on five or six occasions, including in public, at the theater, and in palaces, as well as during my tenure in the army. His people's affection for him was palpable throughout Egypt.

It is imperative to attend to the people of a king before forming an opinion about him.

France is also beloved by the Egyptians. They are fluent in French, possess French credentials, and their culture is inextricably linked with ours. A connection that is worth maintaining.

Massimo Bontempelli: A Poet's Admiration

He composed the following for me: "With immense enthusiasm, following an unforgettable high-art spectacle."

"With immense enthusiasm after an unforgettable evening—a show of true art."

I possess only one word in Massimo's native language: ammirabile.

Italian is a language that is as easy to pronounce as it is to look at. I would opt to reside and pass away in Italy if France did not exist.

Francis Carco: The Poet of Paris Streets

Lu, vu, entendu—"Read, seen, heard."

Francis Carco wanders the sidewalks of Paris with a sly smile that befits a poet, and he is neither a bad nor an unbearable man. He presented me with a book that was inscribed with the phrase "With my deepest respect." He is not overbearing; rather, he is kind. And no, he does not resemble Napoleon.

Michel Gyarmathy: A Talent Awaiting Recognition

Some individuals achieve recognition without demonstrating any talent. Michel Gyarmathy is an example of an individual who possesses talent but has yet to be identified. He moves gingerly, as if he were apologizing for his brilliance, as a Hungarian in Paris. He ought not to.

He is quietly audacious, and his thick crepe soles ensure that he does not make any commotion. He transformed me into Mary, Queen of Scots, and subsequently into Joséphine de Beauharnais, creating a realm of fantasies within the music hall and accomplishing feats that could only be imagined in grand theater.

He is entitled to renown. Rather, he nearly killed me by burying me beneath the weight of his magnificent costumes, only to be resurrected in them.

The Art World: My Complicated Relationship with Paintings

Modern paintings? I am unable to comprehend them. I frequently find myself laughing without understanding the reason. However, I derive pleasure from exploring museums and becoming engrossed in their worlds. Observing paintings serves as a pretext to indulge in daydreams.

I have a preference for Italian masterpieces. Guardi's efforts never fatigue me.

I have participated in portrait photography. I had the opportunity to meet van Dongen at Beaux-Arts, and we occasionally became friends. His paintings appear to be elder than he is, despite the fact that he is modern and wears a beard. This is a positive attribute.

Before the conflict, Jean-Gabriel Domergue depicted me in his painting. Two portraits were transported to the United States, where they sparked a revolution. A woman of color in high society? Outrageous!

I had lost 25 kilograms due to illness by the time he visited me in North Africa. He was visibly disheartened: "Oh, your exquisite buttocks!" "Your exquisite buttocks have vanished!"

A painter who is courteous, but not so gracious in his speech.

Noël Coward: The Man Who Lost His Smile

Noël Coward! Among British troops in Africa, his visage was a beacon of beauty, as it was so English.

Noël dedicated his entire being to the soldiers in the desert, while London's most prominent performers traveled great distances to perform at the battlefront. He was present in a yurt with Vivien Leigh.

Bubbling, flushed, quick-witted, and genial, his smile is freely given. Certain males guard their expressions. Noël Coward permits you to retain his possessions.

Did I encounter Franco? False. Who is his brother? Indeed.

There are rumors that I encountered General Franco in Madrid and that we engaged in a conversation regarding Spain's destiny. Oh, that's right! A more compelling narrative would involve me performing on castanets in Montserrat.

The truth? I encountered his sibling, who serves as the ambassador to Lisbon. A diplomat who is consistently dignified, composed, and well-mannered. An exception.

The Silent Guardian of France: General de Gaulle

I am drawn to males who captivate you with their gaze and whose eyes are emanating a sense of purity. I have no interest in politics; however, General de Gaulle is an exceptional individual.

He consistently appeared distant, as if he were taking a step back to more accurately evaluate an issue. It was as though you were France itself when he gazed upon you. He refused to allow France to be violated. On that matter, he declined to engage with all parties.

He wore a single uniform during the conflict, which was worn thin and ironed hastily prior to meetings.

He was seated in the presidential box with Madame de Gaulle at the Algiers Theater for my inaugural Free French Forces performance. I was summoned by his officer.

I was introduced to his wife by General de Gaulle, who also assigned me his seat.

His position!

Additionally, what about Madame de Gaulle? She is modest and unassuming, and her sole aspiration is to lead a peaceful existence with her children. She donned a simple barrette, flat shoes, and gray yarn hosiery. She addressed me as "dirty little Gaulliste" with an endearing smile.

The Future? A Final Bow, A Song, and a Stage

The features, endless and expectant, are visible beyond the curtain.

Certainly, I will continue to perform, croon, and dance throughout my lifetime. To be alive is to dance. I desire to expire in a state of exhaustion and breathlessness at the conclusion of a melody, but not in a music hall.

I am weary of the artificial and the allure of celebrity. I no longer desire the gaze of the spotlights.

Lena Horne will portray Josephine Baker in a film that the Americans are developing about me. However, I will portray myself. Then, I will abandon the stage permanently.

I will journey to Les Milandes in search of tranquility, family, and a life surrounded by creatures and children.

Finally, Marcel, my poet, I would like to express my final wish:

Record this information.

I aspire to become a faerie. The mythical godmother of a small French village that is situated in a remote location.

Printed in Great Britain
by Amazon